STEVEN J. JENSEN

living the good life

A BEGINNER'S THOMISTIC
ETHICS

THE CATHOLIC UNIVERSITY
OF AMERICA PRESS
Washington, D.C.

LIBRARY OF CONGRESS
CATALOGING-IN-PUBLICATION DATA
Jensen, Steven J., 1964–
Living the good life : a beginner's Thomistic
ethics / Steven J. Jensen.
p. cm
Includes bibliographical references and index.
ISBN 978-0-8132-2145-8 (pbk. : alk. paper)
1. Thomas, Aquinas, Saint, 1225?–1274.
2. Ethics, Medieval.   3. Christian ethics—
Catholic authors.   I. Title.
B765.T54J47 2013
149'.91—dc23   2012043722

For Clare, Louis, and Anna

Magis diligitur quod est coniunctius....
Parentes diligunt filios ut aliquid sui existentes
et ideo dilectio secundum quam pater diligit
filium similior est dilectioni qua quis
diligit seipsum.

(II-II, 26, 9)

CONTENTS

vii

ACKNOWLEDGMENTS

I would like to thank all those who have helped with this book. Those deserving special mention include my wife, Christine, for her constant support and guidance; James Stromberg, who provided the foundation and inspiration; Stephen Brock, Thomas Cavanaugh, and Isaac Block, all of whom provided helpful comments and suggestions; Barbara Stirling for her discerning eye for art; Carol A. Kennedy for her careful reading of the manuscript; James Kruggel for his interest and assistance; Trevor Lipscombe, director of the Catholic University of America Press, for his willingness to undertake the project; Theresa Walker and Beth Benevides for their dedicated work at CUA Press; and my many students over the years.

I

Introduction

You call him a dumb ox, but I tell you this
Dumb Ox shall bellow so loud that his
bellowing will fill the world.
Said of Thomas Aquinas by Albertus Magnus

Knowledge is the food of the soul.
Plato

I once sat on a bioethics panel in which a member opined that he had discovered the most profound insight while watching a documentary in which the closing shot asks the question, "Is there an absolute truth?" The narrator steps down a hill into a swamp and scoops up some of the slime. So standing, he declares, "This is what comes of the belief in absolute truth." Suddenly the shot is transposed and we find that the narrator is standing in Auschwitz. Surprisingly, this member of the panel proceeded throughout the ensuing discussion to give conclusive pronouncements on nearly every topic raised. The profundity of his insight, it seems, had not yet sunk in. Yet surely he expressed an idea that is common stock in our society. While Jesus Christ said, "The truth will set you free," today we profess that the truth will chain you down. It leads not to freedom but to Auschwitz.

It is no surprise that these defenders of relativism are averse to checking some simple historical truths; after all, the truth will only lead them astray. But if they would bother examining the beliefs of Hitler's Nazi party, they would discover little reference to absolute truth, especially ethical truths. Indeed, Auschwitz arose not through any staunch defense of absolute truth but through discarding some fundamental truths, such as the dignity of human life. Nazism came to power in the wake of a decadent relativism; it rallied the people not with promises of a return to truth but with cries of a return to German power. The semiofficial philosopher of Nazism was Friedrich Nietzsche, who recommended that we get beyond the outdated categories of good and evil and turn simply to power. Absolute truth indeed! The horrors of the Holocaust were able to happen only because too many people were willing to discard their belief in the dignity of each human being. Had this absolute truth been lodged firmly in every person's heart, then history would have been rewritten for the better.

Unfortunately, we continue to shirk the truth. When someone proclaims the truth we berate him for being close-minded, insensitive, and judgmental. To remedy his shortcomings, we suggest that he adopt a broader mindset and become open to other viewpoints. After all, every viewpoint is on equal footing; none is better than another. In short, whenever someone asserts something as true, and other things as false, he is seen not as a liberator but as a tyrant, forcing his view upon others.

But not every view is equal to every other, and ideas have

consequences, sometimes deadly consequences. Should we bear with equanimity someone who says that we can kill individuals whose lives are not worth living? Should we blithely ignore those who say we should clone and engineer human beings to create a superior stock? Should we welcome claims that some defective human beings are not people—they lack all moral rights—so that we can do with them as we please? All of these views are being boldly advanced today with little protest. Fundamentally the same views were rampant in Germany in the 1920s and '30s. I fear that we have become indifferent to evil and we pass our indifference off as tolerance.

As history tells us, we abandon the truth at our own risk. With this in mind, I advance one viewpoint as better than others. Not, of course, that Thomas Aquinas has all of the truth, or that others don't have any of the truth. We should welcome the truth where we find it, and we should not close our minds off to plausible viewpoints without some cogent reason. On the other hand, we should also acknowledge the truth when we find it, and we should reject what is false. For this reason, I present Thomas Aquinas as hitting upon much of the truth with little admixture of error. He is a good starting point and a sure guide because he has insight into the truth, of which our society is in desperate need. Not only did Aquinas happen upon true statements; he understood them. He discovered the underlying causes of things, putting everything together into a coherent structure that still stands today.

Who was Thomas Aquinas? He did not lead an eventful life, except in the realm of ideas and arguments. He fought no battles and won no wars. He discovered no new lands, nor ruled over old realms. He neither made a fortune nor invented any new device. But he did win arguments; he discovered new truths, and amassed a wealth of understanding. He was born in Italy in 1225 and died in 1274. In that short time he wrote volumes of tightly packed arguments that remain clear and cogent to our day. While he was a graduate student under Albertus Magnus, his fellow students called him the "dumb ox": an "ox" because he was rather large, and "dumb" because he said very little. As is often the case, however, his silence covered a depth of understanding. Albert the Great recognized Aquinas's genius and retorted that when this ox bellowed he would be heard around the world. And so he was. And so he is still today. For a more complete account of the life of Aquinas, you may wish to read *Saint Thomas Aquinas: The Dumb Ox* by G. K. Chesterton.[1]

Aquinas is adept at uncovering the root causes of things. He is not known as one practiced in the art of political affairs or in directing people's daily lives. Indeed, he passed up a bishopric, preferring instead to contemplate the eternal truths. You might even say he was absent-minded. Once while at the dinner table with King Louis IX of France, he sat intent in thought, ignoring the conversation of those around him. Suddenly, he slammed his fist upon the table, declaring, "That settles the Manichees."[2] Because Aquinas discovered fundamental truths, rather than merely observing worldly affairs around him, his writings are still applicable today. What finished off the dualism of the Manichees in the thirteenth century still finishes off dualism today. We know nothing of that dinner conversation with the king except what Aquinas said about the Manichees.

Aquinas is also skilled at weaving together the thoughts of his predecessors, for he always respected the authority of past

1. For a contemporary edition, see G. K. Chesterton, *St. Thomas Aquinas* (San Francisco: Ignatius Press, 2002).
2. Ibid., 94.

thinkers, even when he differed with them. His writing is peppered throughout with references and direct quotations from Scripture, Aristotle, Cicero, Augustine, Boethius, Averroes, and many others. His memory of these writings must have been what we call photographic, especially considering that he lacked the resources we have today, such as computers. Aquinas himself said that he was given the gift of understanding everything he read. Evidently, he was also given the gift of remembering it.

Despite his erudition and profound insight, Aquinas lived a humble and saintly life. He entered the Dominican order against the protest of his family, who even locked him in a castle for a year, hoping to dissuade him from joining the Dominicans, until they allowed him to escape under pressure from the pope. One story has it that his family tempted him with a prostitute, so that he might abandon his aspirations to the religious life, but young Thomas took a hot fire poker to the woman, who hurried from the room without accomplishing her task.

Aquinas did not overly promote his own work. The last year of his life he quit writing, leaving unfinished his greatest work, the *Summa Theologiae,* from which most of the references in this book are taken. When pressed to write more, he refused, saying that all he had written was as straw compared to what had been revealed to him. Evidently, some mystical experience had so impressed upon him the glory of God that before it everything else paled, even his own works. He was not saying, of course, that all he had written was false; rather, he implied that truths discovered in this life on earth, even the penetration of truth found in his own writings, were insignificant compared to the truth in God himself. If Aquinas's works are like straw, then woe to the rest of us.

In this book we will examine the ethics of Thomas Aquinas. We are merely setting out the basics, providing a starting point that can serve as a foundation for further ethical insight. We will not delve into the details of Aquinas's view, although even the little we will examine reveals an intricately ordered and systematic account. To keep our attention focused, we will not consider disputed and varied interpretations of Aquinas's writings. For the most part, the material in this book is uncontested by scholars of Aquinas, although at times I have been forced to choose one interpretation rather than another. I seek only to give beginners an elementary starting point, from which they can then pursue other writings if they so choose.

In each chapter I use the ideas of Aquinas to address some common views associated with ethics today. The second chapter challenges the common perception that ethics is only about what is right or wrong; the third chapter addresses values clarification; the fourth chapter questions the attitude that we need only do what we think is right (whether or not it is in fact right); the fifth addresses determinism; the sixth addresses a Kantian attitude of "Just do the right thing"; the seventh goes beyond the idea that ethics is simply an examination of difficult and disputed ethical issues; the eighth and ninth chapters address utilitarianism; the tenth addresses situation ethics; the eleventh examines virtues belonging to reason; the twelfth focuses upon the most important of these virtues, namely, prudence or practical wisdom; the thirteenth addresses the question, "How can we know what is right and wrong?"; finally, the fourteenth chapter addresses the question, "Why be moral?" Each chapter might be viewed as showing what Aquinas would say about these topics.

Let me add a short note on the parenthetical references. They direct the reader to texts of Aquinas that address the ideas being discussed. Most of these citations are from the *Summa*

Theologiae, and they consist of three or four elements. The first element is a Roman numeral, or a combination of Roman numerals, such as I, I-II, or II-II. This element identifies the volume of the *Summa*: I refers to the first part; I-II refers to the first part of the second part; and II-II refers to the second part of the second part. The second element consists of an Arabic number and it refers to the question within the volume. The third element is another Arabic number, referring to the article within the question. Finally, the fourth element, when there is one, consists of the Latin word *ad* and a number, for instance, "ad 3," which refers to Aquinas's reply to the numbered objection. For example, if you run across the citation (I, 1, 6, ad 3) then you should look in the first volume of the *Summa Theologiae,* question 1, article 6, at the reply to the third objection.

2

Ethics and the Good Life

Happiness is attained through virtue; a man arrives
at it through his own choices.
Thomas Aquinas

One's virtue is all that one truly has, because it is
not threatened by the vicissitudes of fortune.
Anicius Manlius Severinus Boethius

Perfect Injustice

In the *Republic* Plato has Glaucon build upon an earlier argument of Thrasymachus; he asks us to imagine one person who is perfectly unjust and another who is perfectly just. The perfectly unjust person, he says, will rise to power through unjust means, but because he is so perfect at his injustice, he will never get caught. He will become the ruler of his city, and will have the pick of his wife among the ruling classes. He will be fabulously wealthy and well liked by all, since he is so crafty as to accomplish his injustice without notice. In contrast, the perfectly just person will do what is right no matter the consequences, even when it leads to his own ruin. And it will. For nobody likes a just person; he makes our own injustice all too evident. In the end, the perfectly just person will be persecuted and falsely accused of every sort of injustice. What is more, he will be found guilty of these putative crimes and sentenced to torment and an ignominious death. Upon hearing Glaucon's description, we are led to think not only of Socrates, whom Plato had in mind, but also of Jesus Christ.

Which life, then, asks Glaucon, is the happier life, the just life or the unjust life? The answer is plain. The perfectly unjust person leads a happy life and dies a happy death. He accomplishes all his goals, and all his wants are satisfied. The perfectly just person, on the other hand, leads a miserable life and dies a painful death.

Not for another twenty-three hundred years, from the philosopher Nietzsche, do we find such a ringing defense of injustice and evil. But surely most people, in the evil that they do each day, reason with themselves in some such manner. When someone embezzles from his company, he thinks that doing so will make him happy, while not doing so will leave him in misery; when someone refuses to stand up for what is right, he prefers to be well liked rather than to be courageous but despised; and the man who murders his wife for the inheritance imagines that he will be better off without her. Whenever we act, it seems, we are seeking our own happiness, and we often suppose that our happiness is best served by doing what is wrong rather than by doing what is right.

Thrasymachus and Glaucon, however, do not have the last word, for Socrates proceeds to dissect Thrasymachus's argument, and to argue, instead, that the just life is always the happier life, while the unjust life cannot lead to happiness. Justice, after all, is a virtue or a strength, while injustice is a vice or a weakness. It follows that justice can only help us in leading a humanly fulfilling life, while injustice must cripple our pursuit of happiness.

The Subject of Ethics

For the moment let us not focus upon Thrasymachus's concern—whether the just or the unjust life is the happier—but instead let us ask which of the following two questions best hits upon the topic of ethics: (1) "Which actions are just and which actions are unjust?" or (2) "Which actions are humanly fulfilling and which are not fulfilling?" Most people are apt to respond that the first question is the concern of ethics, while the second question is the concern of some such field as psychology. What everyone seems to suppose is that the two are quite distinct questions. What makes an action good and right has nothing to do with what makes an action fulfilling. It may turn out, as Socrates suggests, that the two overlap, so that just actions are also fulfilling actions, and unjust actions are unfulfilling actions, but in the popular mind the two questions could hardly be more distant from one another.

But not in the mind of Thomas Aquinas. Indeed, according to Aquinas the two questions could hardly be more intimately related. Furthermore, he might well use either of the two questions to delineate the topic of ethics (I-II, 1, 3; I-II, 21, 1, especially ad 2 & 3). Ethics might be described as the study of human actions insofar as they are right or wrong, or it might equally be described as the study of human actions insofar as they are fulfilling or not fulfilling. Between these two, however, the latter has a certain priority.

Suppose for a moment that we forget about justice and injustice and think instead only of the good life. After all, we do want to lead a fulfilling life. Let us consider all of our actions only in one light: insofar as they contribute to the good life. Let us describe some actions as good and others as bad, meaning not that they are morally good or morally bad, but only that they are good or bad for fulfillment.

Such a perspective is not new, for each day we all judge our actions in the light of happiness. Unfortunately, we often make a bad job of it. We judge, for instance, that getting even with our enemy will lead to happiness, but it only deepens our misery. We judge that a night on the town is just the thing needed, but it only leads to a hangover. We judge that buying that extravagant new car will satisfy our wants, but it only leads to the burden of years of debt. We all do whatever we do in order to attain happiness, but we often find only grief. The hope and desire for happiness, it seems, are not enough to achieve happiness. In addition, we must judge rightly of the actions that will truly get us to happiness.

There is a difference, then, between what we aim to achieve in our actions and what our actions actually do achieve. We aim to attain a fulfilling life, but our actions often bring disappointment. We cannot divide our actions into those that are aimed at happiness and those that are not, for all are directed toward fulfillment. We can, however, divide our actions into those that attain fulfillment and those that do not. Even apart from morality, then, we can judge some actions as good or bad in the light of human fulfillment.

By taking such an approach have we abandoned ethics? Not at all. We would be deep in the thick of ethics, which seeks to evaluate human actions insofar as they are truly fulfilling or not. As such, you might expect to find ethics in the self-help section of the local bookstore, for there you may find the dos and don'ts of leading a fulfilling life. Indeed, self-help books are a sort of modern ethics. Even in our relativistic society, self-help books recognize that we all seek human fulfillment; they recognize that not all ways of life are in fact fulfilling; and they offer, as ethics ought to, various prescriptions for a truly fulfilling life. Many self-help books claim to provide us with the skill of living happily well. Of course, they often fail. Still, what they set out to accomplish is nothing other than ethics: the rules and guidelines for living a humanly fulfilling life.

A Human Life

We readily realize that the life of a grasshopper is not fulfilling for a human being. There is more to human life than food and reproduction. Even the life of a squirrel cannot meet the standards of human needs. Better to be a dissatisfied Socrates than a satisfied pig. Why? Because the good life cannot be merely animal life. We are human beings, with the capacity to reason and to love. Mere sensation or pleasure cannot fill up our longings. Somehow or other the use of our minds—and of our human hearts—must be caught up in a truly fulfilling life (I-II, 3, 3). As human beings we should not go through our lives blindly following instinct, doing the bidding of each passing desire. We have the capacity to order and direct our lives according to understanding. We also have the capacity to enter into friendship, to seek more than selfish satisfaction from others.

Underlying the above considerations is the understanding that what we are has something to do with what is fulfilling of us. What counts as fulfilling for a grasshopper cannot possibly measure up to our human needs precisely because we are something more than a grasshopper. Our powers, our capacities, could not possibly be filled up (fulfilled) by the life of a grass-hopper. What we are—that we have the capacity to know, to understand, and to love—is intimately caught up with the sort of life that is fulfilling for us. If we settle for less than fully human activity, if we settle for the mere animal activity of sensation or pleasure, then we have not realized our capacities. Does it follow that we cannot take pleasure or enjoy sensation? Not at all. But these activities must be done in a human way, with our human understanding and desires. An ethical life, then, will be a life of realizing our human capacities.

The human potential movement of the 1960s and '70s made a similar claim, that fulfillment can be found only by realizing our potential. As we will see, however, those involved in the movement missed the mark of the true human potential: they turned to emotions rather than to human reason and will. Still, their attempt was fundamentally in accord with the project of ethics. They sought to differentiate between those actions that are fulfilling and those that are not. They even understood the crucial importance of being human, of our human capacities.

Right and Wrong

Will the ethical life, the humanly good life, correspond with what we often call morality, with the right and wrong of actions? Socrates thinks so. And so does Thomas. It is a way down the road, however, before we can reach this conclusion. We must first better understand two things. First, we must further examine our human capacities. Recognizing that our human understanding is crucial to the good life is only a first step. We must examine more carefully what we as human beings can do and how we are fulfilled in our activities. We will discover three essential elements to our human capacities: reason, emotions, and free will. The difference between these three capacities and the interaction between them will be the foundation of a Thomistic ethics.

Second, we must better understand what is right and wrong. We can begin by noting that right and wrong is not the same as either law or religion, although it is sometimes supposed to be both. Some people say that following the law is right and breaking the law is wrong, so that all of ethics is summed up by the law, or if not by the law, then at least by the prevailing custom. "When in Rome, do as the Romans" is taken to be an ethical maxim. In fact, both the law and custom are distinct from right and wrong. Much of morality is outside the boundary of the law (I-II, 96, 2 & 3). Cutting someone down behind his back, for instance, is wrong, but it is not illegal. It may be wrong to tell a white lie, but no society ever makes laws against it. Such laws, if they were enacted, would cause more disruption than good; they would undermine the freedom necessary for the true moral good that laws seek to promote.

Furthermore, morality and human law are not the same because laws can be wrong (I-II, 96, 4). Laws supporting slavery in the United States did not make slavery morally acceptable. Laws discriminating against Jews in Nazi Germany did not make mistreatment of the Jews morally good. Laws allowing abortion in our own day do not make abortion right.

Morality and the law are certainly related. Ideally, our laws should be founded upon right and wrong (I-II, 95, 2). We should want to make laws that promote what is ethically good. The two, however, are not identical, for what is morally right or wrong is sometimes left untouched by the law, and what is legally permissible or obligatory is sometimes unethical. Much the same point might be made about custom. Both law and custom are good, but they should be founded upon ethics, which comes before both.

Nor is ethics the same as religion. Sometimes people say that their ethical beliefs simply are their religious beliefs, and sometimes it seems as if the Supreme Court supposes that any ethical view is ipso facto a religious view. Again, this notion contains some truth, for the major monotheistic religious traditions all have a strong ethical component. Still, ethics and religion diverge, for we can have religion without a strong ethical component and we can have ethics without religion.

Many religions, especially pagan religions, have no moral code essentially associated with them. The pagan religions of ancient Greece or Rome *presupposed* ethical views—those views prevalent in the culture—but they neither proclaimed these views nor originated them. Paganism, to a good measure, tends to allow a great diversity of ethical beliefs.

You can also have ethics without religion. Every culture advances some ethical standards, and when no particular religious influence is dominant, then that ethics is independent of religion. Great philosophers such as Plato and Aristotle advanced ethical views, which they claimed to discover through the sole use of their reason, independently of any religious revelation. Many atheists have high ethical standards.

In this study we will try to examine ethics apart from the human law and religious belief. Although we will be examining the ethical views of Thomas Aquinas, who himself was deeply committed to the Catholic faith, we will not consider, except incidentally, his religious views. He himself thought that Aristotle had discovered ethical truths, and he taught that everyone can discover the naturally good life, independently of any religious revelation.

Where from Here

We wish to examine human actions in the light of the good life. We wish to see how leading a good life corresponds with the truly just life rather than the perfectly unjust life. We must start with our human potential, for the fulfilling life will be the life that realizes our human capacities. Let us examine, therefore, how our human capacities relate to what is right and wrong. We will begin by considering the often misunderstood relationship between our reason and our emotions.

3

Reason and the Emotions

❧

Let your desires be ruled by reason.
Cicero

If It Feels Good, Do It

We have all heard the saying, "If it feels good, do it," but we probably wouldn't associate it with ethics or morality. Indeed, it seems like a recipe for disaster. Raping feels good to rapists, killing feels good to serial killers, and tyrannizing others probably felt good to Hitler and Stalin. We know from our own experience that what feels good is not always the best, either for ourselves or for others, and what feels good now might not feel good later. A drinking binge might feel good at the moment, but not the next morning. It can feel good to put down others, especially our enemies, but we certainly don't want others to be putting us down. In short, our feelings are rarely the best guide for our behavior. "If it feels good, do it" is the chant of rebellion, not of ethics.

Yet today "If it feels good, do it" has the veneer of respectability, for it is promoted as the very foundation of ethics. Matters are not stated so blatantly, but the idea is the same. Usually, there is talk of "clarifying values" or "decision making." We are told that we must find our own values, and we do so by looking inside. Look inside to what? Our feelings. Children and adolescents are asked, "How do you feel about using drugs?" "What do you think of masturbation?" "What are your feelings on premarital sex?" and so on. Evidently, to find right and wrong we need go no further than our own feelings. While we expect children to learn their math from teachers and high school students to learn their science at school, we think that everyone, young and old, need only consult his emotions or desires to discover ethics. We have now arrived at "If it feels good, it's right."

If you like something, then it is a value to you. If you want to be popular, then popularity is a value for you; if you want to be rich, then wealth is a value to you; if you want a family, then family life is a value to you. Sounds good. But something goes wrong when we talk to the Hitlers or Jack the Rippers of the world: "I want to dominate others, so oppression is a value to me, " or, "I enjoy killing others, so murder is a value to me."

In an attempt to avoid these troubling conclusions, values clarification tells us that not all feelings are of equal worth. We should not be led along by fear of peer pressure, or by a desire to please our parents, both of which are feelings. No, we must find our true feelings, the feelings that come to the surface when we forget about other people, when we consider only ourselves. When we are comfortable with ourselves, filled with high self-esteem, then we can discover what we really want. The moral axiom that we ultimately reach is "If, in high self-esteem, it feels good, then it is good."

It all sounds good (whether or not it feels good), but does it really make any sense? Can we really discover some pristine feelings that rise above the rest to guide us into the way of truth? There are lots of reasons to suppose otherwise. Let us consider just one: the problem of self-deception. As human beings, we have a problem with honesty, not only to others, but to ourselves as well. In fact, we are usually better at fooling ourselves than we are at deceiving anyone else. Long after everyone else can see that the lovelorn girl is being used, she continues to praise the virtues of her beloved. Even after the braggart has lost all his friends, he still thinks he is a lovable guy. When we have uncovered our true feelings, then, how can we be sure that we haven't deceived ourselves? Perhaps our "true" feelings are just what peer pressure demanded of us all the while. Such often seemed to be the case in the 1960s when the human potential movement got off and running. When experimentation in drugs was all the vogue, people suddenly discovered that their "true" feelings sought to experiment with drugs. How convenient that their "true" feelings corresponded precisely with popular bidding. Even supposing, then, that we really do have some pure emotions that could guide us to the truth, it would be a formidable task to discover them, sorting them out from their many counterfeits.

When we are honest with ourselves, we recognize that our feelings, even our most fundamental desires, are not all good. In fact, they are often quite selfish and even malicious. We seek our own gratification, even at the expense of others; we envy others their good, and seek to seize it from them; we glorify ourselves in our self-esteem, always placing others below us. Of course, our emotions are not all bad—we possess much instinctive goodness—but we would be fools to trust our feelings as a guide to what is right and wrong. Some emotions are good, others are evil, and we cannot tell the difference just by looking inside.

When Wanting It Makes It Good

Values clarification says that things become good because we first of all want them. Wealth is a value to someone because he desires to be rich; first he desires money, then it becomes a value. Thomas thinks the exact opposite: something is first of all good and that's why we should want it (I-II, 24, 4, ad 2). We should want money only insofar as wealth is good. When too many possessions detract from our well-being, then they cease to be good. We probably all know someone who is obsessed with his possessions; even though he wants more things, they are not good for him. Similarly, we all know children who have too many toys for their own good, yet they still want more. Just because they want them, does it follow that toys are a value to them? Or should we rather say, as we sometimes do, that these children, if they knew what was good for them, wouldn't want the toys? Unfortunately, like our children, we do not always know what is good for us. We suppose that whatever we want is good.

We can perceive the two approaches in someone who is deciding whether to get a new speedboat. Following values clarification he says, "I really want that speedboat, so it is a value to me." Following Aquinas he says, "That speedboat would really be to my advantage (for relaxation), so it is a good thing for me to want," or alternatively, "That speedboat would only get in the way of more important things in life, so I should not want it."

These diverse approaches involve two different movements between opposite poles. Values clarification begins inside, with our feelings, and moves outside. It begins with some want, and moves to say that the thing wanted is a value. Aquinas's ethics begins with the thing outside, which is good or evil, and it moves into our emotions; it begins with good and evil in the world and moves toward what we should desire. While values clarification says that wanting it makes it good, Thomas says that its being good should lead us to want it.

Of course, we don't always want the things we should. If someone we know gets a great promotion, we should feel happy for her, but instead we might feel envy. We might wish that she hadn't got the new job; we might even begin to wish that something bad happens to her. The point, then, is not that we *do* desire what is good, but that we *should* desire what is good. Indeed, we all sense something perverse in someone when out of envy he begins wishing evil upon others. Something is out of order in his desires; something needs to be straightened out.

Not all our emotions or appetites are good, nor do they make things to be good. Rather, we have to set our emotions in order, seeking what is truly good and shunning what is truly evil. Something is wrong with a man who desires to rape a woman. We do not say that raping is a value to him. Rather, we say that his desires have been perverted; they must be set right. If someone hates members of certain minority races, wishing to exterminate them from the face of the earth, we do not suppose that he just has different values from ours. Rather, we suppose his hate is a defect in character. He has misjudged the true value of things, which is that all human beings are created equal, with a dignity that precludes their being treated like objects. Our desires do not make values. Rather, the true values ought to shape our desires.

Be Reasonable

Reason is the middle man between the good in the world and our emotions, for reason first understands the good or evil in the world and then presents the good as an object to be desired. Suppose, for example, that in exchange for a hundred-dollar bill a teller at a bank hands me six twenty-dollar bills instead of the five she should. I am presented with a moral choice. Should I point out the error or pocket the money? Were I to consult my feelings, as values clarification would recommend, I would likely pocket the money. My true desire, I might say to myself, is to have a little extra cash, and only fear of reprisal and disapproval pushes me in the direction of returning the money. Thomas, however, says I should not consult my feelings. I should consult reality. Quite apart from my feelings, the truth of the matter is that one of these actions is good and the other evil. As I stand there looking at the money with my hand held open, I know what I should do. How do I know? With my reason, for reason perceives the true good and evil in reality.

But how does reason know? That is a difficult question, which we will address later. For now, we can at least recognize *that* we know some things are right and others wrong, even if we don't understand *how* we know they are right or wrong. We know that rape and murder are evil; we know that racism is wrong; we know that helping out a friend in need is good; we know that ruining someone's reputation by backbiting is evil; and we know that returning the extra twenty dollars is only fair. Ethics certainly has its fair share of difficult questions—what are we to do about capital punishment, how should we justly distribute the wealth of the nation, when can someone in great need take what belongs to others, and so on—but why should we start with these troubling cases? Let us begin with what we know. Most of the moral decisions we make in a day are rather straightforward. We know the right thing to do, even if we don't end up doing it. Embezzlers who are caught indicate that a class in ethics wouldn't have helped them because they already knew that taking the money was wrong. For most of our decisions we don't need college-level classes, or even high-school classes, to tell us what is right. We already know. We know it through our reason. *How* do we know? We will see later. For now let us be content in realizing *that* we know.

Let us return to the bank. I stand there, holding the money in my hand, and with my reason I recognize that I should return the extra twenty-dollar bill. What is going on in my emotions at the time? I might very well resent the judgment of reason, coveting that extra money. But recall that Thomas says we should desire the true good. What I should be desiring, then, is to return the money. Unfortunately, since I am less than perfect, I might still desire to pocket it. Still, I should recognize that this desire is out of order; it is not the way things ought to be. The desire to pocket the money is not a value generator, somehow making theft to be good; rather, it is opposed to the true good recognized by reason.

We can now trace the movement of values clarification, and the contrary movement proposed by Aquinas, through the three points of the world, reason, and the emotions. Values clarification begins in the emotions, with a desire in our hearts. It then moves to reason, for we must become *aware* of our values or our wants. Although values clarification doesn't mention reason, we will assume that we become aware of our wants with our mind, or with our reason. The final step, when we call something good, moves out to the world. For example, I might move through the three steps as follows: (1) I begin by desiring to pocket the money; (2) I am then aware that I want it; (3) I finally declare that taking the money is good.

According to Aquinas the movement is reversed. We begin with reality, for some things are really good and others really evil. We move to reason, which is aware of the good and evil in things. Finally, reason presents the true good to the emotions as an object of desire, and (hopefully) we desire it. First, the truth is that returning the money is the fair thing to do; second, I am aware of this true good; finally, I desire to return the money. Of course, in my imperfection I may not reach this final step, but we should acknowledge that my errant desire to steal is indeed an imperfection, rather than the source of my values.

The emotions or desires, then, do not generate right and wrong but are instead judged as right or wrong, as reasonable or unreasonable. We do not want something, as values clarification would have it, and then it becomes a value to us. Our true emotions are not always good, just waiting to be uncovered. Rather, we must use our reason to discern which emotions are good and which evil. Reason perceives the good and evil in things, and so it perceives the good and evil in our emotions. This teaching of Aquinas is reflected in our common intuition that we should be reasonable. We often become irritated with others when they express some unreasonable emotion, such as uncontrollable fear, blind infatuation, or smug pride. Why? Because we suppose that emotions should be reasonable. When others step beyond the plane of reason, we want to bring them in line. If only we were as adept at discovering our own unreasonable emotions.

Rationalization

As I hold the money some thoughts quickly run through my mind: "The bank has more than enough money; they will never miss it"; "It was *her* mistake, after all, not mine"; "I've had some hard blows lately, I could use a little break"; and so on. What I am doing is rationalizing. I am considering taking the money, but I feel uncomfortable about it, so I try to soothe my conscience with quasi-moral justifications. The idea that I should follow the moral judgments of reason is so grounded within me that I want at least the appearance of being rational. I am doing that at which we all excel, deceiving myself.

As the name would suggest, "rationalizing" has something to do with reason, and so we must distinguish it from the role of reason that we have already identified, namely, understanding the true good and presenting it to the desires. Let us consider what happens in my rationalization. I begin by realizing that I should return the extra twenty. This step is necessary, for if I did not realize that pocketing the money was wrong, then I would have no need to soothe my conscience. Although I initially recognize what I should do, I nevertheless desire to steal the money, for I think it would be nice to have a little extra cash. In other words, with my desires I am not following the judgment of reason. I am going off on my own, against the true good, to strike out toward a good of my own making. Still, I feel uncomfortable following my desires, for reason insists that taking the money is evil. To assuage this discomfort I now enlist reason in another role, justifying my evil desires. A rationalization, then, has three steps: (1) we begin by realizing what is truly right and wrong; (2) we desire what is wrong; and (3) we come up with quasi-moral reasons for following our evil desires.

Notice that the last two steps of rationalizing are surprisingly similar to values clarification. Rather than have our emotions follow reason, we submit our reason to our errant emotional desires. Values clarification says, "I desire it, therefore it is good for me." Rationalization says, "I desire it, therefore, find some way that it is good." Precisely this role reversal—making reason the servant of the emotions—marks rationalization. The proper order of things, according to Aquinas, is that reason perceives the good, and then the emotions follow. One's mental house is disordered when the reverse is true. Of course, consulting our emotions is often appropriate. If I prefer chocolate ice cream to vanilla, then I may go along with this desire. Choosing between flavors of ice cream (usually) has no moral significance; since reason recognizes this fact, following my desires in such a decision is perfectly rational. Reason is still in control, for it says that the true good allows the emotions their sway. On the other hand, when our emotional desires are opposed to the true good perceived by reason, then we should not submit to the desire; rather, the desire should submit to reason.

The self-deception of rationalization, then, places our emotions above our reason. No wonder, then, that values clarification is so open to self-deception. In search of our "true" emotions we simply follow the lead of whatever desire seems compelling. We do not use our reason to sort out between our emotions, judging some as good and others as inappropriate, for that would presuppose some standard that reason discovers; it would deny the primacy of the emotions.

We find, then, two possible movements within Aquinas, the movement of morality and the movement of rationalization. The movement of morality begins in the world, with the true good in things; it then passes to reason, which perceives the good and evil. Finally, the emotions pursue the good presented to them by reason. But because our emotions or desires sometimes go their own way, departing from the good of reason, there also arises the movement of rationalization. This movement begins with the emotions that have some desire (we will see that it begins even earlier, in the imagination). The emotions then induce reason to find some value that corresponds with the desire.

Reason and the Emotions

We have discussed the ethical relationships between two mental powers, reason and the emotions. We should note some distinctive features of each. First, we should note that we are using the word "emotions" rather loosely, to refer to any felt desire, aversion, enjoyment, sorrow, and so on. This usage corresponds to Aquinas's idea of the passions of the soul. Unfortunately, the English word "emotion" is not a perfect fit for Thomas's "passion." We are not inclined to call a desire for pizza an emotion, although it is a passion of the soul. Still, "emotion" is the best word we have; we don't need to stretch the word too far in order to include desires for pizza. Just be aware that as the word is used in this book, it includes all varieties of felt desires.

Reason is a knowing power, while the emotions are what Aquinas would call an "appetite" (I, 79; I, 80). As a knowing power, reason takes in the world, perceiving the way things are. We make all sorts of judgments with our reason, most of which have nothing to do with ethics. For example, scientific judgments about the nature of things involve the use of reason; atoms, fields, and black holes are all grasped through the use of our reason. On a more ordinary basis, our judgments that someone is angry, happy, or sad all depend upon our reason, for we do not see anger; we see a person's behavior, such as shouting, and we conclude that he is angry. Our judgment that certain foods are healthful and others unhealthful depends upon our reason. Even a simple judgment such as that things subsist and continue in existence depends upon reason. We are so accustomed to our use of reason as it interplays with the senses and imagination that we hardly separate reason from these other powers. Consequently, we have a tendency to anthropomorphize animals, attributing to them the same mental judgments as we ourselves have.

Among the things that reason judges are the good and evil in reality. Reason goes further, taking on a kind of active role, for it seeks the means of attaining the good. For instance, after I have judged that I should return the money, I then make a rapid judgment that I can attain this goal by saying to the cashier, "I think you gave me one extra twenty." That example is rather simple, but suppose I have judged that getting a college degree is the right thing for me. I then have to discover how I can get the degree. I look into various colleges, comparing their strengths and weaknesses, I apply, and so on. Indeed, this constructive reasoning is likely to go on intermittently over long periods of time.

In contrast to reason, the emotions make no judgments about the world. They do not take in the world, but move out to it. Anger, for instance, is not a judgment about someone; it is an attitude toward someone, an impulse to act in a certain way. If Mary is angry at David, then she does more than judge that David has been unfair (although she does do this); in addition, she is propelled to act toward David in certain ways: yelling, making a sarcastic comment, and so on. We have a rich array of emotions, including desires and aversions, sorrow and joy, gratitude and envy, fear and daring, hope and despair, and many more.

English lacks a good word to cover all of these emotive impulses. For convenience, we will use the words "desire" or "appetite" as generic terms to cover all emotions. Anger, then, will be a certain kind of desire, meaning simply an impulse to act.

According to Thomas, emotions are shared with the animals, while reason is found in human beings alone (I-II, 24, 1, ad 1). Anyone who has had any experience with higher animals, such as dogs or cats, will know that they experience joy and sorrow, desire and aversion, fear and anger. On account of the interplay between reason and the emotions, some emotions may be peculiar to human beings, such as envy, which is sorrowing over another's good fortune (I-II, 24, 4, ad 3). Even envy, however, might have some counterpart in animal behavior.

On the other hand, reason is found in human beings alone. Other animals do share some amazing mental capacities with us, such as the senses, memory, and imagination, but we should not submit slavishly to bold scientific pronouncements that animals such as chimpanzees have reason just like us. We have not space to go into a discussion of the matter, but we need only note that a very little observation reveals a dramatic difference between human and animal behavior. We don't find animals doing mathematics, using technology, composing music, painting art, inquiring into the realm of outer space, and so on. If, then, we find animals doing rather amazing things, we should not rush to conclude that they have reason, just a smaller portion than our own. Rather, we should acknowledge that they do have some mental capacities, but the gulf between animal behavior and human behavior indicates something entirely new, the light of reason.

Finally, we should note the relation between reason and the emotions. By presenting an object of desire, reason can direct the emotions to the true good (I, 81, 3). Aquinas teaches that we cannot desire something unless we first of all know it (I-II, 27, 2). You cannot desire pizza unless you first call to mind some idea of pizza, however dimly. You cannot fall in love with someone unless you know something about him or her. Furthermore, knowing merely chemical facts about pizza will not generate desire; you must have some idea of the pizza being good, in taste or nutrients or some such thing.

As we have seen when we looked at rationalization, the opposite sort of movement also takes place: the emotions can suggest to reason that an object is good. I judge that a new red sports car is good only because my desires pull me along to the judgment. As we will see, these diverse movements of the emotions and reason will play a large role in the moral life.

Which movement leads to true human fulfillment? That which begins with reason, with human understanding and judgment. "If it feels good, do it" is poor advice for happiness. Human fulfillment is much more than feeling good at the moment, for our emotions are often misguided. People have spent months, years, and whole lifetimes seeking to gratify perverse or twisted desires; they have wasted their human capacity of reason upon the plotting of revenge or upon the destructive fulfillment of envy. Even if we search for our "deepest" emotions, our supposedly true and natural feelings, we are still in the dark without reason. If we do not use reason to judge our emotions, then we are apt to elevate to the level of "natural" whatever desire seems most pressing at the moment, which will, as often as not, lead to our downfall.

Rather than placing reason at the service of the emotions, we should seek to desire rationally; we should seek to humanize our emotions. True human fulfillment means having true human desires, not mere animal impulses. We are more than instinctive beings; we can act with foresight and understanding. Why should we cast our human capacity of reason down to the level of a slave, following the blind impulses of our passions? Should we not, rather, raise our emotions to the level of reason, directing and guiding them with insight? Can we, as rational beings, be satisfied in any other way? Can we be satisfied merely by gratifying our impulses?

4

Conscience and Choice

*Every judgment of conscience, be it right
or wrong, be it about things evil in themselves or
morally indifferent, is obligatory.*

Thomas Aquinas

Whatever You Believe

Have you ever heard it said, "All that matters in ethics is that
you do what you believe to be right"? Or "Just follow your conscience"? Seems like sound advice. Unfortunately, too often the
seed of truth within these sayings is distorted into a denial of
all morality. If all that matters is that we do what we believe,
then why do we have to bother studying about ethics, about what
other people believe? Why should we turn our attention to the
"true" goods "out there," when all we need do is consult our own
internal beliefs?

Indeed, how can we speak of some objective good in reality
when one person's beliefs differ from another's? Teresa believes
that lying is wrong; Martin thinks it is a good thing. Both are

doing the right thing just so long as they follow their consciences. What, then, are we to say about the morality of lying? Is it right or wrong? Well, that all depends upon what you believe. It's right for Martin and wrong for Teresa. The objective goods in the world disappear; all that remains is what appears good to Teresa and what appears good to Martin. Apparently, then, if we accept these two sayings, then all morality becomes relative to each person's particular beliefs.

But the trouble with both these sayings is that they are too expansive. *All that matters* is that you do what you believe. *Just* follow your conscience. If we remove the words "all that matters" and "just," leaving "Do what you believe" and "Follow your conscience," then Aquinas can agree with these statements; they contain an element of truth, but they are not the whole truth.

Voluntary and Involuntary

Suppose you witness a man shoot and kill a little girl. You would be horrified. But then it transpires that he had been hypnotized to believe that the girl was a ferocious bear attacking him. It turns out that he was only saving his own life. He was doing what he erroneously believed to be right, so he should not be blamed for his action. This example appears to confirm the above dicta: the man is not doing something morally wrong, since he is doing what he believes is right. This example, however, can also be the basis for realizing what is wrong with these sayings.

In what sense did the man kill the girl? Certainly the bodily activity he performed was an act of killing a little girl. On the other hand, he did not really choose to kill a girl. What he chose to do was kill a bear. The activity of killing the girl, in fact, was against his will, for had he known it was a girl, he would never have fired.

Our actions can be against our will, or involuntary, in two ways, either through coercion or through ignorance (I-II, 6, 5 & 8). This example exhibits the second, for the man is unaware that he is killing a girl. The police dragging you to prison against your will is an example of the first, for you go to prison against your will. Both share a common feature: namely, the action does not arise from the person's will but is in opposition to it (I-II, 6, 5). Being dragged to prison is opposed to what you actually want right now, while killing the little girl is opposed to what the man would have chosen, if he had known what he was doing. Voluntary actions, on the other hand, are in agreement with a person's will and arise from it (I-II, 6, 1). Clearly, your act of going to prison arises from the police and not from your own will. Similarly, the act of killing the little girl does not arise from the man's will but is in opposition to it. What arises from his will is an act of killing a bear.

Suppose you were not dragged to prison, but threatened with beating if you did not comply. You still go to prison (we would say) *against your will*. Nevertheless, Aquinas says it is not against your will, or involuntary, in the fullest sense (I-II, 6, 6); it is involuntary only in some respect, for in this instance you do want to go to prison in order to avoid a beating. Why, then, do we say that it is *against your will*? Because we must distinguish between what is generally against your will and what is against your will right here and now. Generally speaking, you do not want to go to prison, but in the particular circumstances right here and now you do want to go to prison, if only to avoid pain and injury. The action, therefore, is voluntary but may be called "against your will" in some respect.

Ignorance causes involuntariness because every act of will presupposes knowledge of what is to be done. Before you can choose to buy a car, you must know what it means to buy a car; before you can want an education, you must know what an education is. When the required knowledge is lacking, we can perform actions against our will.

Matters are not so simple, however, for Thomas distinguishes between three kinds of ignorance, or three ways ignorance might relate to an act of will: concomitantly (together with), consequently (following upon), and antecedently (prior to) (I-II, 6, 8). Ignorance is *together with* an act of the will in the following situation. Pat is out hunting and he sees a deer through the trees. He takes aim and fires, but unknown to Pat, his worst enemy, Dan, is hiding in the distance behind the deer, so that when the deer leaps away, Dan dies rather than the deer. Upon hearing a scream Pat investigates and discovers Dan giving out his last breath. He smiles contentedly and walks away. This ignorance is concomitant with Pat's will because the action he performs in ignorance, killing his worst enemy, is in accord with his will. He would have done it even if he had known. This sort of ignorance gives rise not to an involuntary action, which is against someone's will, but to a nonvoluntary action. It does not arise from his will, but then neither is it against his will.

The second sort of ignorance, consequent ignorance, follows upon an act of will, and so it might be called *voluntary* ignorance, ignorance that is in some manner chosen. Suppose, for example, that Pat knows another hunter is somewhere about the forest, but he is not sure where. Upon seeing movement in the trees, he quickly shoots without bothering to check whether it is a deer or a man, for he does not want to miss his opportunity. He shoots in ignorance of his target, but that very ignorance is something that he wanted, or at least that he did not want to overcome.

35

This *voluntary* ignorance is often rather indirect; we want to know, or at least we are not opposed to knowing, but we just don't want to know badly enough (I-II, 6, 8; I-II, 76, 4). We prefer something else to informing ourselves. Suppose that a doctor has a patient with an unusual condition and is spending his afternoon reading up on her symptoms. Then a friend drops by and asks to go out for a drink. While the doctor knows that he really should find out more about the illness, he decides to take a break and have a drink. He spends the whole afternoon and evening with his friend, and never gets back to his studies. The next day when he sees his patient, he is not prepared to treat her. His ignorance follows upon an act of will, for he chose not to study. Nevertheless, he did not *want* to be ignorant; he just wanted a good time with his friend more than he wanted the knowledge. Such ignorance should be called *indirectly* voluntary (I-II, 6, 8; I-II, 76, 3). In contrast, when somebody actually wants to be ignorant, then his ignorance is directly voluntary, for instance, when someone chooses not to find out a law because he wishes not to follow the law.

Suppose the doctor mistreats the patient. Is his act of mistreating according to his will or against his will? In a sense, says Thomas, it is against his will, for the doctor surely does not want to mistreat patients. In another sense, however, it is voluntary, for his desire to treat his patient well was not strong enough; when forced to choose between informing himself and drinking with his friend, he preferred the latter. Ultimately, says Aquinas, an action performed in consequent ignorance should be called voluntary; it is involuntary only in some respect.

Finally, antecedent ignorance precedes the act of will. Here someone is ignorant of what he has no need to know, or of what he has had no opportunity to inform himself. Actions following upon this ignorance are indeed involuntary. The man who was hypnotized had no possibility of discovering that the bear was really a girl, so he kills the girl against his will.[1] A hunter who does all that he can to discover whether another human being is in the vicinity of his target but nevertheless ends up shooting someone has done so against his will.

Blame and the Involuntary

What does this discussion have to do with Martin who wants to lie and Teresa who does not? Each follows his or her conscience; each does what he or she believes is right, so it seems that lying is right for Martin but wrong for Teresa. Similarly, the man kills the girl believing he is merely killing a bear, so the act is right for him.

Consider that we do not blame someone for what is involuntary (I-II, 21, 2 & 3). If while in prison you are not fed for three days, we would not blame you for neglecting your health, for your failure to eat is against your will. Nor do we blame the man who is hypnotized (supposing, of course, that the hypnosis was itself not something he chose), for while he does an evil deed— he kills a little girl—he does not know that he is doing it. Since his act is involuntary, we do not blame him for it. This idea of assigning blame only for what is voluntary also seems to underlie the notion of an insanity plea. Suppose someone commits murder and then pleads insanity. He is not claiming that his action of killing was good; he acknowledges its evil. Rather, he is arguing that he should not be blamed for the evil he did. Why? Because he was insane (at least temporarily), and so could not truly choose, making his action involuntary.

1. Although in I-II, 6, 8, Aquinas mentions only ignorance of what one is not bound to know, in I-II, 76, 3, he also mentions invincible ignorance.

This idea of withholding blame for evil deeds allows us to distinguish between objective wrongdoing and subjective blame.[2] An act may be objectively wrong, truly evil in the nature of things, and yet someone may not be subjectively to blame, if he performs the act involuntarily. We don't really need to speak, then, of something being right *for him* or wrong *for him* based upon his belief. We can say, rather, that killing little girls is simply wrong, in the very nature of things, and yet sometimes a person should not be blamed for killing. We might say that it is *subjectively* right for him, as long as we understand that the rightness does not apply to the act itself but to the responsibility of the one performing it.

The example of lying is a little different, for Martin lies voluntarily. He knows full well that he is lying, and no one is coercing him into the act. Still, if we grant that lying *is* wrong, so that Martin is mistaken in his belief, we can discover something that Martin does involuntarily (supposing that his ignorance of the truth is antecedent to his will): Martin lies voluntarily, but he does evil involuntarily. He fully realizes that he is lying, so the act of lying is voluntary. He does not realize, however, that he is doing evil (for he believes lying to be good). Since antecedent ignorance gives rise to involuntary actions, Martin, who is ignorant of the evil of his action, does evil involuntarily.

Once again, then, we can distinguish between what is objectively right and what subjective blame should be assigned (I-II, 19, 5 & 6). According to Thomas, lying is by its nature an evil

2. The notion of objective wrongdoing, in opposition to subjective blame, is not Aquinas's manner of speaking. A more precise Thomistic way of making the distinction is to distinguish between the evil of an act considered in itself and the realization of that action in the concrete. This account is given in chapter 10. The current account, however, may be derived from Aquinas's discussion of an erring conscience, in which he distinguishes between the good and evil of the action considered in itself and the good and evil as understood by reason (I-II, 19, 5).

action; objectively speaking, telling the truth is good and lying is evil. Given Martin's ignorance, however, we should not blame him for lying, for he does not realize that it is evil. If we must speak in the manner of being right *for him,* then we should say that lying is evil of itself but subjectively all right for Martin, who is doing what he believes is right.

Need we say, then, what was suggested at the beginning of this chapter? Because Teresa believes lying is wrong and Martin believes it is right, does it follow that there is no objective truth to the matter? Not at all. Teresa is correct in her belief and Martin is incorrect in his. Nevertheless, we might not blame Martin for lying, and in that sense we can say lying is right for him. It is not, however, *objectively* right for him; rather, he should not be *subjectively* blamed for lying, since he has antecedent ignorance of the true evil of lying.

Conscience

Still, the two sayings, "Just follow your conscience" and "All that matters is that you do what you believe is right," remain untouched. Lying may be objectively wrong, but Martin should still follow his conscience. Indeed, the objective right or wrong of the matter seems to have no bearing upon his behavior, for no matter what is really right, he should just do what he believes. When it comes to practical decisions all that matters is subjective blame; objective right or wrong is irrelevant. So it seems. But is it? As we will see, something more is needed beyond following our conscience; in addition we must also *inform* our conscience.

Our conscience is our judgment of what is right and wrong. We say, "Teresa's conscience says that she should not lie" or "Martin's conscience says that he should lie." In both instances, "conscience" refers to a judgment about whether lying is morally good or evil. Of course, we judge other actions besides lying. Our conscience includes judgments about killing, stealing, abortion, sexual activity, and so on. But conscience means more yet, for we can make two sorts of judgments about right and wrong. We can make the general judgments that we have discussed so far, such as "abortion is evil," or "helping the needy is good." But we also have concrete judgments about what we should do here and now. Right now I should help this person out. I should not abort my child. And so on. Both of these sorts of judgments—the general rules and the concrete decisions—can be called conscience. We say, "My conscience says I should not steal," but we also say, "My conscience says I should give this money to charity." Between these two, Aquinas prefers the latter usage, in which conscience refers to our concrete judgments, but he grants that we sometimes use the term to refer to the more universal judgments (I, 79, 13). Our modern English usage is looser. We apply "conscience" as readily to one judgment as to the other.

Our conscience, then, is our judgment about what is morally right and wrong, either generally or in the here and now. We must also understand an erroneous or misinformed conscience, which is a conscience that makes the wrong judgment (I-II, 19, 5). Martin's conscience is misinformed, for he incorrectly judges that lying is all right. Someone who thinks that slavery is all right also has an erroneous conscience. His judgment does not agree with the reality of the matter, which is that slavery is evil. Someone who judges he can kill certain minorities simply because they are minorities also has a misinformed conscience. What he thinks is good is in fact evil. Whenever a person's judgment opposes the true good or evil in things, then he has an erroneous conscience.

We can understand what is insufficient about "Just follow your conscience" by examining two interesting questions about a misinformed conscience: First, "Are we morally obliged to follow an erroneous conscience?" (I-II, 19, 5). Second, "Are we excused for following a misinformed conscience?" (I-II, 19, 6).

If our conscience is correctly informed, then it seems unproblematic to say that we are bound to follow it, but what if our conscience is misinformed? Suppose Roger is a young man growing up on a plantation in the antebellum South, and his conscience tells him that he should keep slaves, for having been told such from his infancy, he has never doubted it. What should he do? Should he follow his conscience, even though it leads him to do the evil of keeping his slaves? Or should he go against his conscience, so that at least he would be doing what is right?

Thomas answers that he should follow his conscience, for we are obliged to follow our conscience. If Roger goes against his conscience, he might happen to do what is right—free the slaves—but he would not know it is right, for the very idea of an erroneous conscience supposes that we are unaware of our error. If Roger knew he had a misinformed conscience, then he would know that slavery is evil, and if he knew slavery was evil, then his conscience would be correctly informed. Someone with a misinformed conscience, therefore, does not realize his own error. He might, perhaps, suspect that he does not know all that he should; as we shall see, he might at some previous time have known that his knowledge was inadequate, although even then he would not have known his exact error.

Aquinas says we must follow our conscience, because our conscience is our only contact with morality. Even when erroneous, it is our only foothold in what is right and wrong. To reject our conscience, then, is to reject morality. It is to say that we do not care about doing what is good. If Roger rejects his erroneous conscience, he is rejecting what *he judges* to be right. He is saying, "The heck with doing the right thing."

What of the second question? Does a misinformed conscience excuse us for doing wrong? If Roger follows his conscience, keeping his slaves, then should we excuse him even though he did what is objectively wrong? Should we blame him for doing what he thought was right?

The answer to this question is not straightforward. Does an erroneous conscience excuse? Sometimes yes and sometimes no. It all depends upon what sort of erroneous conscience one has. Recall that ignorance can be either consequent or antecedent (we will ignore concomitant ignorance for the current discussion); it can either follow upon an act of will or precede an act of will. Similarly, either an erroneous conscience might follow upon an act of will, and so be voluntarily misinformed, or it might be prior to an act of will, and so be involuntarily misinformed.

Someone has a voluntarily misinformed conscience if he has had a reasonable chance to correct his error but he did not take the opportunity. Suppose, for example, that some abolitionists are visiting the nearby town. Roger considers going to hear what they have to say, but then changes his mind; he would rather play chess. Notice that he had an opportunity to correctly inform his conscience, but he passed it up. His conscience is indeed misinformed, but he himself is to blame for that misinformation. His conscience, then, is voluntarily misinformed.

A voluntarily misinformed conscience does not excuse. If Roger continues to keep slaves, then we should not excuse him for doing wrong. Why? Because he voluntarily got himself into a state of confusion. He is like the doctor who prefers to drink rather than learn about his patient's condition. The error he makes is voluntary and blameworthy because his ignorance is consequent upon his choice to go drinking. Similarly, Roger's ignorance about slavery is consequent upon his choice to play chess rather than to discover what is right or wrong.

In contrast, an involuntarily misinformed conscience does excuse. Someone has an involuntarily misinformed conscience if he has had no reasonable chance to correct his error. He is left in what Aquinas calls invincible ignorance, ignorance that cannot be overcome (I-II, 76, 2). In the extreme case, the person doesn't have any opportunity at all to discover the truth. Roger grows up in such a sheltered life that never is it hinted that slavery might be wrong. In a less extreme case, an opportunity presents itself, but it is not a *reasonable* opportunity. The person could find out, but other obligations prevent him. Roger, for instance, considers going to see the abolitionist, but on the appointed day his mother falls ill and he must care for her. He is presented with an opportunity, but it is not reasonable, for the obligation to care for his mother should take priority. We are perhaps more sensitive to this sort of thing than Aquinas and his age were. Nevertheless, Aquinas does speak of ignorance of what one is not obliged to know. While he does say that everyone is obliged to know the universal moral norms (such as that slavery is wrong), it might come to pass that this obligation is impossible to fulfill, perhaps because of more important obligations, such as taking care of one's mother.

Needless to say, determining whether a certain misinformed conscience is voluntary or involuntary is no easy task. Reality is not so simplistic as I have presented it above. The state of someone's conscience is a judgment better left to God, for we do not know what is going on in other people's thoughts.

In contrast to a voluntarily erroneous conscience, an involuntarily erroneous conscience does excuse (I-II, 76, 4). The person is not responsible for his confusion, so he should not be to blame. He is like a doctor who did all that he could to discover the nature of the illness, but nevertheless erred in his judgment. We would not blame him for his mistake, for his error was not voluntary.

The two kinds of misinformed conscience can be compared to two ways that a person might be drugged. The first person chooses to take the drugs himself, for the thrill of it, and while in his stupor he kills someone. Claiming that he was confused is no defense, for he voluntarily got himself into that state of confusion. He knew that he might end up doing something terrible as a result of his drugged state. Similarly, someone who has a voluntarily misinformed conscience has got himself in a state of confusion, so it is no excuse to say that he didn't know it was wrong.

On the other hand, the second person does not drug himself but is drugged by others, who slip a pill into his drink. When he ends up killing someone in his stupor, then he might well protest that he was confused and did not know what he was doing. For him, the killing was indeed involuntary; the confusion was itself antecedent to his act of will. In contrast, the person who drugs himself kills voluntarily (though the killing was involuntary in some respect) because the confusion was consequent upon his act of will. An involuntarily misinformed conscience is like being drugged by others. It does excuse, for the state of confusion is in no way chosen.

The person with a voluntarily misinformed conscience is in an unfortunate state. If he does not follow his conscience then he has done wrong, for we are all bound to follow our conscience on pain of abandoning morality. On the other hand, if he follows his conscience he does wrong as well, for he is not excused for the evil he does. He is damned if he does and damned if he doesn't. He can get out of this unfortunate predicament only by doing what he should have done from the beginning: inform his conscience (I-II, 19, 6, ad 3).

We must all do precisely this—inform our consciences—lest we end up in the same boat. The saying "Just follow your conscience" is not enough. In addition we must correctly inform our consciences. It is no excuse to say, "I was only following my conscience," if I have not first put in the effort to assure that my conscience is correct. In our society we are rather complacent about our consciences. We figure that they are in order, and we need not bother about them. We would rather sit down and watch a television sitcom than bother thinking about ethics; we are no better off than Roger who preferred chess. According to Thomas we should indeed be concerned with informing our consciences. If we do not, then we are left in the uncomfortable position of being unable to do good; damned if we do and damned if we don't.

Yes, we should follow our consciences. Yes, we should do what we believe is right. But that is not all. We also must inform our consciences. We must strive to believe correctly. We must seek to know the true good and evil in reality. Only so can our conscience be founded in the truth; only so can we attain what is good in the nature of things. We should not go about our lives duped by a kind of complacent hypnosis that leads us into evil deeds. We should reject the error of hypnosis for the truth of reality.

Conscience and the Good Life

What do voluntary and involuntary actions, informed and misinformed consciences, tell us about a humanly fulfilling life? Perhaps only what is patently obvious. Our human fulfillment is realized not through some physical process but through voluntary actions. Having a good digestive tract might contribute to a good life, but the act of digesting well is not itself a humanly fulfilling act. Were we to go about our lives in somnambulance, standing and sitting, eating and drinking, and even talking, but all the while in the deepest of slumbers, we would hardly be leading the good life. The mere physical processes of standing, walking, eating, and talking do not constitute the human good. These activities must be human, which is to say they must be voluntary and deliberate. What happens to us fortuitously, quite apart from our choices, may often contribute to our happiness, but a life of good luck absent conscious and voluntary activity would be empty. The domain of ethics coincides with voluntary actions precisely because human fulfillment can be realized only through our actions.

Part of acting voluntarily, we have seen, involves knowledge, for ignorance detracts from the voluntary. The good life, then, requires that we know what we are doing. We should not wish to remain in ignorance, doing blindly what in fact may be harmful to our well-being. It would be a tragedy if we went about lying, or abusing people as slaves, all because we were ignorant that these activities are opposed to the happy life. The good life, then, demands that we should inform ourselves, that we should seek the truth about what is good and what is evil. It is not enough that we should do what we think is right; we must also think rightly. We must know the good, for only then can we do it.

5

Loving and Choosing

*Those who have reason have freedom to will or
not to will, although this freedom is not equal in
all of them. Human souls are more free when they
persevere in the contemplation of the mind of God,
less free when they descend to the corporeal, and
even less free when they are entirely imprisoned
in earthly flesh and blood.*

Anicius Manlius Severinus Boethius

Deterministic Behaviorism

The will plays a central part in the moral life, and yet many people want to deny that we have a will. They say that we are merely complicated animals, whose emotions are less inborn and more learned than in other animals. Nevertheless, they are inborn, and they are learned. We have no choice by which we can influence our emotions; we have no freedom by which we can get beyond our genes and our environment. We are fixed and determined by our heredity and our upbringing. What we desire

47

we must desire; what we do we must do. Such are the claims of deterministic behaviorists, who point to various influencing factors upon our behavior. Growing up in a family with alcoholism trains a child to behave in one way; growing up in poverty trains a child to behave in another; and growing up in wealth yet another. These children, and the adults they become, must act as they act. Their emotional dispositions are fixed, not through their own choices but by the forces that have acted upon them.

In protest against this view, some thinkers, including Aquinas, point out that without a will and choice, no actions are voluntary, and if actions are not voluntary, then a person cannot take responsibility for them. He is to be neither praised nor blamed for what he does. Further yet, it makes no sense to tell him what he ought to do, for his behavior is determined anyway. Ultimately, morality itself makes no sense, for if we are not free to choose, then we can do neither good nor evil (*De Malo* 6).

Deterministic behaviorists respond by claiming that morality is just one more environmental force that can be used to control other people's behavior. Telling a person that he "ought" to tell the truth might in fact get someone to tell the truth. Behaviorists further argue that rewards and punishments make sense without freedom, for they too are tools to control people. We reward a child for sharing because we seek to make him share in the future. We punish someone for theft because we hope to influence him or others so that he will not steal in the future.

On this rather bleak worldview, morality is nothing more than manipulation. Of course, some behaviorists attempt to sound high-minded and suggest that we should use our manipulation to create a world of plenty and happiness. But why bother? Why shouldn't we follow the trend of human history and try to make a world in which we are rich and powerful at the expense of others? Behaviorists cannot say that we "ought" not, for we recognize that ploy (morality) as simply a form of their own manipulation.

We won't dwell upon the argument. Instead we will turn to Aquinas, who thinks that as human beings we are indeed free on account of our will, a power distinct from either the emotions or reason.

A Choosing Power

Perhaps we cannot really *prove* that some particular action is free. If I claim that I have freely chosen to return the extra twenty-dollar bill, then the determinist will insist that it was my heredity, or my environment, that fixed my dispositions such that I was determined to return it. Unless we were to realize every causal factor involved with my choice, a feat impossible to the human mind and very far removed from our present knowledge, we could not say with absolute proof that any given human action is free or determined.

Aquinas thought that, in a more general way, we could show that as human beings we have the capacity for free actions. Since we have reason, and can perceive diverse ways of achieving our goals, it follows that we are not always determined in our actions. We will not, however, dwell upon this rather difficult argument. Rather, we will provide certain indications of our freedom, the first of which is common experience. We all daily experience making choices, choices that are up to us. We know firsthand that we ourselves determine what we are going to do; we all know that we could have done otherwise. This common experience gives us a fair definition of freedom. We are free when we can determine for ourselves a course of action. Our action is not determined by something outside ourselves, such as heredity or environment, nor is it purely random or uncaused. Rather, we ourselves determine what we will do.

A second indication comes from observing human behavior and contrasting it to animal behavior. If we observe animals in the wild (and not in captivity), then we see that they follow very set patterns of behavior. Of course, as we go higher in the animal kingdom, we discover a greater variability of behavior. Snakes exhibit greater variety in their behavior than do worms, and chimpanzees exhibit more than snakes. The variability of behavior in even the highest animals, however, is constrained within the boundary of a set pattern of behavior. When we get to human beings, however, we find a sort of explosion of variability. Of course, we are not free from patterns. But the variety within human cultures and between human cultures far exceeds anything found in the animal kingdom. This variety is no proof of freedom—it might arise merely from a greater complexity—but it is an indication of freedom. Freedom serves as a kind of best explanation for the variability of human behavior.

A final indication arises from the intimate connection between freedom and morality. Without freedom, morality makes no sense. Exhorting people, praising them, blaming them, and so on, are meaningless if we are determined (I, 83, 1; *De Malo* 6). We can, of course, turn exhortations and morality into a kind of manipulation, as the behaviorists would have it, but then we have perverted their original sense. We all know that we reward someone because he deserves it, and he deserves it only if he is free; we punish someone because he has it coming, which could not be if he were forced to behave as he did; we tell people what they ought to do only because we know they are free to do as they please.

Someone might protest that we cannot possibly be free since

we act in predictable ways. All of us have certain habitual patterns of behavior, either inborn or developed through our life, that lean us heavily toward one behavior rather than another. An alcoholic, for instance, is apt to take another drink, since he has developed such a strong disposition towards alcohol. A teetotaler is likely to refuse a proffered drink in accordance with his habit. Similarly, an irritable person will predictably snap when you bother him, and we know that a shy person will blush when standing before a group of people.

The above objection, however, arises from a misunderstanding of free will. It supposes that freedom is indifference, when in fact it is indetermination. By indifference we mean that someone does not care one way or another about two or more options. I am indifferent between buying a silver or a white car, because I don't care which I get. By indetermination we mean that someone is not necessitated to act in a certain way. I am not determined to choose the silver car because my heredity and environment do not necessitate my decision; I myself must make the final determination.

The mistake is to suppose that indetermination is the same as indifference, to suppose that I cannot be undetermined about my choice unless I am also indifferent. Then a habit of the will would preclude freedom, for a habit implies the opposite of indifference: a strong inclination in one direction rather than another. If I have a habit of choosing to eat chocolate ice cream, then I am far from indifferent about it; I care very much about the chocolate ice cream. But, the argument proceeds, if I am not indifferent, then I am determined in my choice and I am not free.

Fortunately, there is no good reason to suppose that a strong inclination necessitates choice. I might be strongly inclined to choose to eat the ice cream, yet I am not determined to do so;

51

I can still choose otherwise, although a habit makes the opposite choice more difficult. If I have a habit of giving in to my sexual desires, then choosing against them will be very difficult, and the stronger the habit the more difficult the opposite choice becomes. But never does it become impossible. My freedom remains intact.

A Spiritual Power

At any rate, whatever arguments might be presented on either side, Thomas certainly thought we were free, and the seat of that freedom lay in the will, with which we choose. The will is distinct from the emotions, which would indeed be fixed and determined were we not free (through our reason and will) to consider matters in a different light. While the emotions are shared with the animals, both reason and will are found only in human beings. They are spiritual powers rather than bodily powers (I-II, 17, 7). They elevate us above the material world, giving us a dignity not found in any other physical being.

The bodily nature of emotions is revealed through another name we sometimes give them, namely, feelings, for emotions are indeed something that we feel. Since they are bodily desires, they involve some bodily change (I-II, 22, 3). When we are fearful we tense up and our hearts beat quickly; when we are embarrassed, blood flows to our faces; when we are sexually aroused, our bodies change accordingly. We become aware of these bodily changes at a sensible level, and so we "feel" our emotions. A boy who is infatuated feels a transformation inside him when the girl he fancies walks into the room. When we are happy we feel sensibly different than when we are sad. Emotions, then, although they are mental powers, are mixed with the body and are called feelings.

The will is different. It is not at all bodily but purely spiritual (I-II, 22, 3). Its act involves no corresponding bodily change, and consequently we cannot become aware of it at a sensible level. Of course, we are aware of it. But we don't *feel* our choices the way we *feel* our emotions. I am aware that I have chosen to reject the proffered desert, but my awareness is much more intellectual, involving reason rather than the senses. Unfortunately, because of this somewhat intangible nature of the will, we tend to ignore it. We dwell upon our emotions, which clamor for our attention. We end up satisfying the demands of the body while forgetting the demands of the soul.

A Loving Power

This forgetfulness is more harmful than we know, for the will is much more than a choosing power; more fundamentally, it is a loving and desiring power. I choose to reject the pleasure of ice cream because I first desired, with my will, some other good, such as the good of losing weight. Every choice presupposes some desire, and if it is the will that chooses, then it is also the will that desires. Of course, I might desire with my emotions also. I might be emotionally ashamed of my profile; I might emotionally covet the popularity that I imagine arising from a trimmer figure. But if I am to choose, then the desire must go beyond these emotions; with my will, as well, I must desire to lose weight.

We are apt to be skeptical of such desires. After all, we do not feel them. We are quite palpably aware of our shame; the longing for popularity is tangible; but the longing of the will is not sensed. Why suppose, then, that such desires exist? Cannot the emotions explain all that we do, as the behaviorists would have it?

No, they cannot. Some of our behavior exhibits a love and desire deeper than the emotions. Consider, for example, the behavior of good men and women. Mother Teresa cared for the sick and dying even when her emotions cried out against it. Father Damien De Veuster, the so-called leper priest, spent the last years of his life with the lepers of Molokai. His activity was often emotionally repulsive. He cared for the open leprous wounds and endured the stench of decay. There was nothing in it for his emotions, and yet he persisted. He loved with a deeper love than the emotions.

We need not go to the saints to find this love—although in them it is more clearly manifested—for in our own lives also we can see the love of the will in action. Any true friendship goes beyond mere emotional attachment. Indeed, we all know that friendship is tested precisely when the emotions go by the wayside. In times of trial, when emotionally we want to abandon our friend, we nevertheless stick it out. How? With a love of the will. Marriage is a particularly clear example of this love of friendship, for the married couple is bound to stick it out through all the emotional upheavals. The initial warm feeling of romantic love can often give way to irritation, anger, and even disgust. A good marriage, however, will ride over these stormy emotions. Every marriage, of course, falls short of the ideal, but most marriages have a portion of the ideal, in which we can see a love deeper than the emotions at work. A marriage founded only upon the feeling of romance is doomed to failure.

The desires of the will, of course, do not always oppose emotions. Within marriage, the desires of the will and of the emotions are often in harmony. The point of drawing attention to the opposition is simply to indicate the need of some desire beyond the emotions. We are not merely feeling beings; we are animals with more profound desires than emotions. Unfortunately, we are apt to neglect these more important desires. The urgings of the emotions are ever before our minds, making one demand after another, and we run about satisfying them, forgetting the yearnings of the will. In time our wills fall in line, abandoning its higher aspirations for the petty satisfactions of the feelings. Yet even in this degeneracy, the pining of the will rears itself. Why must we always have the television going, or music playing? Why must we always busy ourselves and never rest a moment in silence? Because we cannot bear the silence of solitude, where the true emptiness of our lives is revealed. We prefer the noise, so that we can forget how desolate our lives truly are. The deep dissatisfaction that resides in our wills must not be given the opportunity to show itself.

True human fulfillment demands that we seek to satisfy more than our passing desires. We should not follow the lead of whatever desire seems most pressing at the moment, for the emotions may *appear* more pressing merely because they are felt. We should, rather, seek to satisfy our most profound longings, the desires of our will, where we find true love and true joy. Satisfaction is found not only in bodily pleasure. We enjoy good novels, fond moments with friends, and the delight of coming to understand a difficult point. The more lasting satisfaction is found in the will, not in emotional gratification. As human beings we are much more than feeling beings. We can know and understand; we can love with a spiritual love and delight in the goods of the spirit. Happiness cannot be found simply in satisfying our various emotional desires, whatever they may be. Our human makeup prevents such a relative happiness, which differs from person to person depending upon what desires he or she may have. What we are—spiritual beings with spiritual capacities and wants—affects what fulfills us. Mere emotional satisfaction cannot fill up the human heart. Such is the wisdom behind John Stuart Mill's statement that "it is better to be a human being dissatisfied than a pig satisfied; better to be Socrates dissatisfied than a fool satisfied." Not just anything can fill our human capacities. Only a human life, a life of reasoned desire, will truly satisfy us.

Will, Reason, and Emotions

We now have three players in the moral life: will, reason, and the emotions. We have seen that the emotions should follow the lead of reason but that sometimes reason is led along by the demands of the emotions. Now let us consider how the will fits into the picture. The will is like the emotions in that it is a loving or desiring power rather than a knowing power. While reason takes in the world, the will and emotions move out to the world (I, 81, 1). The will is also like the emotions because we can desire nothing in our wills unless we first understand it as good (I-II, 27, 2). The will, however, is even more tightly tied to reason than are the emotions, for the emotions can be led not only by the judgment of reason but also by some pleasant presentation of the imagination (I, 81, 3, ad 2). Someone might be sexually aroused, for instance, simply from an image, without an intervening judgment of reason. That is why our emotions arise spontaneously, even in opposition to reason. In contrast, the will cannot be stirred to desire without reason; the senses or imagination alone will not suffice (I, 80, 2), for the will is the appetite of reason, even as the emotions are the appetites of the senses. It follows that we can desire nothing with our will unless we first understand it as good with our reason (I-II, 8, 1).

Since reason understands the true natures of things, including the nature of the good, the appetite that follows upon it, namely, the will, desires what is good precisely insofar as it is good. The emotions, following upon the perception of the imagination, desire this or that particular kind of good, such as good-tasting food or a good reputation. In contrast, the will desires goodness itself or complete goodness. With our wills we desire the good and then seek some particular good thing in which the good is realized. All that we desire is desired under the formality of the good.

People choose evil, of course, and even in a manner they desire evil, but they do so only insofar as they perceive it as good (*De Malo* 1, 3). Someone might murder his mother for the inheritance. He has desired and chosen the evil of murder but only because he thought it was good; that is, he thought it would make him rich. Someone else might commit adultery, which is an evil, but he desires it only insofar as he thought it was good for pleasure.

This last example helps us understand the relation between the will and the emotions. For among the goods perceived by reason is the satisfaction of the emotions (I-II, 9, 2). Satisfying my longing for chocolate ice cream is a sort of good, even if pretty minimal. An emotion, then, can make something appear good, even when the same thing, in the absence of the emotion, does not seem good at all. Accosting my friend Bob usually does not seem good to me, but yesterday he offended me, and the resulting anger makes confronting Bob seem appealing. Why? Because it satisfies the urge of anger.

The will, then, is led on by the satisfaction of emotions as a possible object of desire and choice. Nevertheless, the emotions do not force the will to act (I-II, 77, 7).[1] They transform an oth-

---

1. The individual is determined by his emotions only in the case of insanity, but in that case Aquinas says not that the will is coerced but rather that there is no act of will (I-II, 77, 7).

erwise uninteresting object into something appealing, perhaps very appealing, but they do not determine the will. If a married man is sexually aroused by another woman, then adultery becomes appealing, but it does not become necessary. The emotion of sexual arousal does not force or coerce the will in any way; it merely draws on the will. Sometimes you hear it said that a man has arrived at "the point of no return," meaning that he is so sexually aroused that he can't turn back. But of course he can, and if an earthquake struck, he certainly would turn back. He doesn't need anything so dramatic as an earthquake. All he needs is strength of will, for he is not bound to choose what his emotions lead him toward.

Ultimately, the will is in charge, for we do what we choose and we choose with our wills. The emotions can sway us one way or another, but the final word is with our choice (I, 81, 3). We are not, as the behaviorists suppose, mere creatures of conditioned impulse; we are rational beings with rational desire. Much of the moral life will involve resisting the emotions with their tempting presentation of apparent goods. We must recognize the true good with our reason and love it with our wills. Along the way we may have to endure the dissatisfaction of our emotions. We must have the strength of will to hold fast to our true human fulfillment, ignoring the cravings of the emotions, which seek not the true good but only their own gratification. With time, their protests will lessen, and a well-ordered peace will reign within. We must remember that the emotions are more independent of who we are—they arise spontaneously even in opposition to our wishes—than is the will, which expresses our deepest desires. How unfortunate, then, that we readily suppose the opposite, that we are what we feel. Rather, we are most of all what we do, and we do what we choose with our wills. Of course, the will is not just some power within us; it *is* us. It is we who choose, as it is we who reason and we who feel (I, 77, 1, ad 4). Of these three, we most express ourselves through our wills (I, 48, 6). Therefore, it is not just our wills that choose; it is we who choose.

6

Doing Right and Desiring Right

I count him braver who overcomes his desires than him who
conquers his enemies; for the hardest victory is over self.
Aristotle

Do the Right Thing

We haven't yet discovered whether I took the twenty dollars or returned it. Recall that the teller gave me the extra twenty; with my reason I judged that it was fair to return it, but in my emotions I longed to keep it, so that I was beginning to rationalize. What, ultimately, do I do? Do I stuff the bills in my pocket or do I resist the temptation? In the end, someone might insist, all that matters is that I do the right thing. No matter how much I am tempted to take the money, no matter how much I delay in rationalizations, it does not matter as long as I reject these temptations and return the money. That is the bottom line of the moral life, doing the right thing, for we cannot always be expected to desire the right thing, but we are all required to do the right thing.

This approach, while correct, does not encompass the whole

truth. The moral life is more colorful than this grim bottom line would suggest. Yet, "Do the right thing" is a common view expressed in our culture today, and it was the rallying cry of a great moral philosopher by the name of Immanuel Kant, who lived in Konigsberg, Germany, from 1724 to 1804. He was a brilliantly systematic philosopher, who developed an intricate view of the world that fit neatly together like a jigsaw puzzle, and he initiated the moral theory called deontology. He had a lot to say about morals, and much of it very good. We will see more of him later on, but for the moment we want to concentrate only upon his central teaching of "Do the right thing."

Kant and Aquinas shared some common notions. Like Aquinas, Kant recognized the role of reason in knowing the truths of morals, but he gave to reason a more active role. While for Aquinas reason discovers the goods that are out there, for Kant reason constructs right and wrong. Then too, Aquinas and Kant shared a similar attitude toward the pernicious influence of disordered emotions, which Kant called inclinations. Both thinkers thought that it was largely the emotions that lead us astray to choose what is evil. Kant may have taken a more pessimistic attitude about the inclinations than did Thomas. For Aquinas, the emotions are something of a mixed bag, sometimes good and sometimes evil, but for Kant the inclinations are nearly always bad. Even if they incline us to do some good deed, such as helping someone in need, they do so in a selfish way, for we end up helping the person only for our own satisfaction. According to Kant, about the only good inclination is a respect for the law, that is, an inclination to do the right thing because it is the right thing to do. Inclinations are always separate from reason. In contrast, for Aquinas the emotions can be informed by reason.

To combat these errant inclinations Kant introduces the will, by which we can choose to do the right thing even against our emotional desires. If nothing else, the will is our power to choose, to determine our course of action. Should I return the extra cash? That is up to me; it is my choice. Since I choose with my will, the will is like the very heart and nerve of who I am; I can have all kinds of turbulent emotions roiling about inside of me, but the real me is what I choose in my will (1, 48, 6).

A good will, then, is of primary importance for the moral life. It is the very foundation of Kant's ethics, and it certainly has prominence in Thomas's. For Kant, the notion of a good will is summed up by our phrase "Do the right thing." Regardless of our temptations, regardless of our rationalizations, what matters is that we do the right thing. We do the right thing by choosing, and we choose with our wills. Therefore, all that matters is that we have a good will.

Or is there more? Perhaps, we should not only choose rightly; we should desire rightly as well. Not only should I choose to return the money. I should want to return it.

Self-Control and Losing Control

Consider another situation. I have determined that I must lose ten pounds and that I should do so by going on a rigorous diet. Now a friend offers me a large portion of ice cream with strawberries and chocolate syrup. The friend will not be offended if I refuse, but on the other hand, it is my favorite dessert. What do I do? My reason insists that the dessert is unnecessary and that it is opposed to the needed diet. My desires are clamoring for satisfaction, longing to taste the ice cream. How is this internal battle resolved? We all know that it can be resolved either way, and that what I do is up to me. I can choose to side with reason or with my desires.

Notice how I might describe each choice after the fact. If I choose to eat the dessert (for companionship, I tell myself), then I am likely to go home that night and berate myself for "losing control." "Why am I always so weak?" I might say to myself. On the other hand, if I decline the dessert, I will congratulate myself: "I controlled myself," and "I showed strength of will."

As the philosopher Plato noted long ago, this manner of speaking is rather odd. Why should I say that I lost control when it was I myself who made the choice to eat the ice cream? If I lost control, then who had control? Was my body moving without my consent, consuming the ice cream while I protested from within a mental prison? Of course not. It was I who ate the ice cream and I who was in control from beginning to end.

Yet Plato claims some truth may be found in this manner of speaking, for *reason* loses control. If I side with my emotions, then I dethrone reason from its seat of control. Of course, the opposite is also true: if I side with reason then I take control away from my emotions. In either event, I give control to one of the warring factions within me. True, but Plato insists that we say, "*I* lost control" because we identify more with our reason than with our emotions. Reason is the higher part, says he, for reason is a spiritual part found only in human beings, while emotions are shared with the animals (II-II, 155, 1, ad 2).

And do not all but the most libertine of us agree? We associate much more with the steady judgments of our reason than with the passing and fickle yearnings of our emotions. I say that "I lost control" because I see myself more as a man who has decided to go on a diet than I see myself as someone who happens at the moment to be desiring ice cream. The language of controlling ourselves and losing control, then, confirms Thomas's idea that our emotions should conform with reason, for reason perceives the true values, and apart from reason our emotions are blind. The good life is found in vision and understanding, not in blind feelings.

Desire the Right Thing

Let us return to the bank, where a similar battle rages within me. Reason has judged that I should return the money; my emotions want to keep it. What do I do? Once again, I can side with reason or with my emotions. Once again, my choice, made through my will, will determine my action. Once again, I am weak if I give in to my feelings, but strong if I choose with reason. Now let us suppose that I do the right thing. Though the temptation was great, I resist it and return the money.

I have carried the Kantian standard. I have done the right thing, regardless of my inclinations. I am certainly to be commended, but could I have done better? Not on Kant's ethics. Nothing is better than doing what the law of reason says I should; by resisting inclination I know most clearly that I have kept that standard. But on this point Kant and Aquinas part ways. Aquinas would grant that I have done the most essential thing; as Kant would say, I have done my duty. Nevertheless, I have not done it as well as I might have, for it would have been better if I had never longed to take the money. It would have been better if I had never hesitated, if I had wished with my will as well as my emotions to return the money, so that I gave it back eagerly, rather than with a tinge of regret. In other words, for Aquinas, strength of will is a good thing but not the whole perfection that we should seek. We should seek not only to choose well, but also to desire well (I-II, 24, 3; II-II, 155, 4).

A host of protests will arise. Our emotions are just a given. We have no control over them. They arise spontaneously, apart from our choices. Therefore, we should not be judged by how we feel, but by how we act. If someone happens to have good emotions, then he is just lucky. Most of us are not so lucky. We want to take the money, to eat the ice cream, and to do many others things that we should not. Still, we shouldn't be blamed for these desires. They are just the way we are made. What matters morally are the choices we make, not the desires we happen to have. Thomas, the accusation claims, is setting up an impossible ideal, for we cannot always desire well. Indeed, he is urging us on to a hopeless battle, a war against emotions that will always be there, that we can do nothing about, and that we should just learn to accept. Otherwise, we are likely to plunge ourselves into a misery of low self-esteem and self-condemnation.

Thomas has really touched a nerve, something dear to our culture, but let me suggest that what he is touching is our complacent mediocrity. We have indeed learned to "accept" our imperfections, so much that we almost consider them perfections. We are quite pleased with ourselves the way we are. Hardly a true acceptance when you think about it, for acceptance implies something unpleasant to be borne. If you win the million-dollar lottery, we are not likely to hear you saying, "I must learn to accept it." The statement seems incongruous, for your prospects are in no way unpleasant. Unfortunately, we all too often have become quite pleased with our imperfections; they aren't *that* bad, after all.

This whole controversy hinges upon the control we have over our emotions, for if we have no control over our emotions, then we should accept them the way we should accept the weather. If we have some measure of control, however, then we can take our emotions into our own hands and set them in line. We can still accept our imperfection as something we will never wholly overcome, but we need not sit idly by. A person who struggles with math need not suppose that nothing can be done. He may never be a whiz at math, but he nevertheless can learn something. We are wearied by people who paint their lives black and then mope about, insisting that nothing can be done. Yet when it comes to moral imperfections in our emotional life, we take a similar attitude, claiming that our emotions are a brute fact, to be dealt with like the weather.

But are they? Not according to a long moral tradition before Kant (I, 81, 3; I-II, 17, 7). In this tradition our emotions are considered pliable, both at the moment and in the long run. Of course, we cannot simply turn our emotions on and off, the way we flick a light switch; furthermore, our emotions often arise quite spontaneously, apart from any immediate choice we make. I get angry not because I sit down and decide, "Now is the time to be angry." Rather, some situation irks me and the anger arises, independently of my will. Then, once I am angry, I cannot simply decide not to be.

Still, I can do *something* about it. Consider Thomas Jefferson's advice, "When angry count to ten before you speak. If very angry, count to one hundred." Isn't that doing something about your anger? And sometimes it works; sometimes it calms you enough to think a little more coolly. Of course, it doesn't always work, but nevertheless we can have some measure of control over our emotions.

The control that Thomas recommends is rational control. Remember that reason perceives the true good in reality, and remember that the emotions can respond to the true good that reason perceives. Thomas recommends, therefore, that we think about the object of desire in a different light, in the light of reason (*De Veritate* 25, 4). If I am angry because the person in front of me is driving too slowly, then I control my anger by considering the offense—driving too slowly—in the light of reason. I can admit that in the big picture this offense is small, that in fact it will not inconvenience me all that much, and that I myself am not a perfect driver. These considerations are likely to diminish my anger, if not eliminate it. I have, then, exhibited a measure of control over my emotions.

The emotions do not fall completely under the control of reason because they respond quite spontaneously to the presentations of the imagination (I, 81, 3; I-II, 17, 7). Upon seeing sexual imagery, someone's emotions are aroused by the mere appeal in the imagination. Indeed, in animals the emotions respond only to imagination, but our human emotions also respond to the considerations of reason. Rationalizations, which try to get reason to justify what we desire with our feelings, let the emotions follow the imagination, seeking to subject reason to the imagination. Rational control seeks to direct the emotions by forming the imagination with reason.

This approach will not always work: sometimes our emotions simply will not submit to the judgment of reason. They are too strong and the presentation of the imagination is too lively to give way to the deliberations of reason. Then, indeed, we are in the Kantian boat. We must ignore our emotions and do the right thing. Sometimes, when our desires are very strong, such as with certain sexual desires, the best thing is to flee. Do not engage in battle with these fierce emotions but turn and run, for the courageous person acknowledges when he has met his match.

A Little Freud

This self-control is distinct from what we now call repression, which is not control at all but a kind of denial. Consider again the ice cream case. Suppose that I resolve the conflict between reason and the emotions in the following manner: "Although I want the ice cream I will stop desiring it; the ice cream may taste good, but I will not desire it." This manner of thinking might be slipping into something like repression. Thomas does not recommend this coercive control over our emotions; instead, he suggests that we draw our emotions on with what is truly good. Rather than deny myself this pleasure, which I acknowledge to be good, I should realize that it is good in some respect but bad in another. Rather than simply rejecting the good of pleasure I should focus on the good of self-control or the good involved in my diet. Similarly, while in the bank I should not lie to myself, saying, "I'm not the sort of person who wants other people's money, so I will do the right thing and return the money." I should admit that I *am* the sort of person who wants other people's money, but I should focus upon other things that I want as well, such as being good and upright. Then I have true acceptance of my emotion. I have acknowledged my weakness, and yet also acknowledged my ability to control my emotions.

We all know that repressing our emotions only makes them return with a vengeance. They become so demanding that they must have their way. Neither reason nor repression can any longer stand in their path. Compulsive personalities have often worked themselves into a vicious cycle of repression and release. For this reason, psychologists sometimes recommend simply giving in to our emotions, going with the flow. This approach has some merit, but not when our emotions oppose reason. If a man continually desires to commit adultery, it is not sound advice simply to follow his desires; but neither should he repress his desires. Rather than either of these extremes he should control his emotions with reason. Such control will have the opposite effect of repression; it will not aggravate the emotion but will slowly bring the emotion in line. After years of rational direction, what was once a frequent desire will fade away to be replaced with a new emotion.

In the Long Run

This change of emotional dispositions is nothing other than the development of habits. We are all familiar with habits, many of which are quite trivial, such as flicking off a light switch as we leave a room. We have habits of talking, habits of walking, and habitual facial expressions, but Thomas is concerned with habits of thinking and desiring, habits of reason, will, and emotions (I-II, 49).

We acknowledge such habits in people when we describe their character. We say Peter is hot-headed, meaning that he habitually gets angry; Mary is generous, meaning that she habitually gives of herself; Mike is honest, which refers to a habit of telling the truth; Hilary is arrogant, meaning that she habitually overrates her own good qualities and diminishes others. In short, whenever we describe others' characters we are describing their habits of thinking and desiring.

A habit is a strong disposition to behave in a certain way (I-II, 49, 3). A habit of anger is a disposition to get angry easily; a habit of fear is a strong disposition to be fearful; and so on. A habit does not mean we are determined to behave in a certain way, but acting in that manner is certainly easier. An angry person will not *necessarily* get angry, but it is his spontaneous reaction when he feels slighted. Nor does a habit mean that we can't control our emotions. Even an angry sort of person can use rational control to lessen or eliminate his anger.

We all know that bad habits are difficult to overcome. Fortunately, the opposite is true as well: good habits are difficult to lose. We overcome our bad habits with great effort by repeatedly acting against them (I-II, 51, 2). People who want to quit smoking (which is really more than a habit; it is an addiction. In a strict sense—and the word "addiction" is often used loosely to refer to a very strong habit—an addiction involves a dependency upon some outside chemical, such as nicotine) must repeatedly refrain from smoking. With time, resistance will become easier and easier. Why? Because their old habit is weakening and a new one—of denying themselves a smoke—is forming. Similarly, an angry person can become relatively calm by repeatedly controlling his or her anger. Over time the anger will lessen and become easier and easier to control.

We can't change our habits by simple force of will, as if I could make a New Year's resolution, "Starting January 1, I will be a patient person." It simply will not work, and such an attitude is likely to lead to repression rather than rational control. Rather, changing our emotional habits is a long-range plan. It will take years and years, indeed, a whole lifetime, to replace our old habits with new ones. Nevertheless, change is possible. New habits are developed by repeated behavior.

Habits are somewhat like a path through a field of tall grass. Taking the path is the easiest way, although striking out on another trail is still possible. Similarly, following our habits is easiest, but we are not determined to do so. If we repeatedly take another route we will discover the grass becomes trampled down, so that the new trail is a bit easier. With further use the grass is flattened, and it is easier yet. Finally, the grass dies and we have a whole new path. In the meantime the old path, having become overgrown with grass, is no longer the easy way to go. Similarly, we can strike out on a new trail of our behavior. If we are angry, we can control our anger; if we are stingy, we can give generously. Over time the new behavior becomes easier and easier, until it becomes the dominant habit—our second nature—and the original habit is the more difficult behavior.

Although habits of the emotions are our present concern, we should not suppose that they exhaust the significant habits. Reason and will also have habits. The will is a loving and desiring power, so with it we can be more or less inclined to various goods, depending upon the dispositions that we have developed. One person might have, in his will, a habit of desiring pleasure as if it were good; another might have a habit of desiring knowledge as a good. Within marriage, fidelity to one's spouse can be a habit, as well as that deeper love we discussed earlier. Since we choose with our wills, the habits of our wills are more important than the habits of our emotions. From a habit in the emotions I might spontaneously get angry, but as long as I have not made a choice concerning the anger, I still have not performed a voluntary act, and I am not to blame for the anger. On the other hand, if from a habit of the will I give vent to my anger, or dwell upon my anger, then I have entered the domain of moral blame.

Reason, too, can be habituated in its thought. Since reason is not a desiring power, however, its habits do not so readily lead to activity; they give the capacity to act but not necessarily the exercise (I-II, 56, 3). For instance, a mathematician might be said to have a mathematical habit, which means that he has the ready capacity to think about mathematics. Whether he chooses to use that capacity depends upon his will.

Changing Our Very Selves

Thomas actually speaks of two ways that we can control our emotions, either through reason or through the will (I, 81, 3). The control of reason, we have seen, modifies the emotion itself. What of the control of the will? It turns out that the control of the will is nothing other than what we have called self-control. It means choosing on the side of reason against the emotions. In short, it is in fact a control not of our emotions but of our actions. At the very least, says Aquinas, we need not act out on our emotions. Rational control may fail; we may not successfully modify the emotion itself. Still, we are not our feelings. We do not have to succumb to our passions. We can keep the reins of control.

Even this control of the will, which leaves the emotion intact, can help us in changing our emotional habits. At least such control prevents our emotions from strengthening. For years many psychologists recommended that we give in to our emotions in order to cool them off. We should, for example, vent our anger, because then we will calm down. This bad advice has proven ineffectual. In the short term, of course, giving in to the desire satiates the emotion. In the long run, however, it only feeds the habit. We should not advise a glutton to eat, so that he can calm his desires; although immediately satisfied, the desires will only be strengthened. We should not pamper a spoiled child, so that his temper tantrum is abated; his anger, having been triumphant, will only return redoubled at a later time.

The control of the will over the emotions, then, at least does not feed the emotions; it keeps the emotional habit from increasing over time. Realistically, it probably diminishes the habit somewhat. The habit that is never fed will begin to languish and waste away. Ultimately, the control of the will, which is a control of our actions, aids the control of reason, which is the true control over the emotions. The two together will shape new habits. Old desires will diminish; new desires will be nurtured. Through effort, we can change who we are. From being angry, we can become calm; from being fearful, we can become daring. Our emotions are not fixed in stone but can be shaped through our own efforts.

Response to the Objections

Let us consider, then, the objections to Aquinas's position raised earlier. We can distinguish three objections: (1) we should not be blamed for our emotions, for they are beyond our control; (2) someone with good emotions is just lucky, and so should not be congratulated for them; (3) Aquinas is setting up an unattainable ideal that will only lead us into a hopeless battle, when instead we should just learn to accept our emotions. We will reply to each objection in turn.

First, our emotions are not entirely beyond our control. They are not brute facts but may be controlled—within limits—at the present moment and in the long run through the development of habits. Our emotions often do arise spontaneously, apart from our choices, and such involuntary desires are not blameworthy. When faced with an annoyance, I might spontaneously react with anger; this initial surge of anger may be beyond blame, since it is not voluntary (though if my habit of anger is itself my fault—something that I have consciously developed—then even this first surge of anger may be partly blameworthy). What matters is what I do with this anger. Do I give way to it, nurturing it and enlarging upon it, even though it is unreasonable? Or do I try to direct it rationally?

73

Second, there may be a degree of moral luck, good or bad, in our emotional dispositions. To a large degree our emotional dispositions are inborn (I-II, 51, 1). Some people are born more fearful, others more cheerful, others more angry, and so on. Laid upon this initial disposition is the influence of our upbringing, which may heavily slant our emotions in one direction or another. Growing up in an abusive household is likely to develop a whole different set of dispositions than growing up in a loving environment. Insofar as these emotional dispositions are not voluntary, we are not to blame for them. Nevertheless, we should not forget that our dispositions are not wholly forced upon us. Choice plays a part, for once an emotion arises we choose to react in some way or other. Aquinas may be more likely to emphasize the role of will in habit formation than we, who are ever aware of the influence of nature and environment, yet we should still acknowledge the place of will.

Finally, when we say that we should not only choose rightly but also desire rightly, we mean that we should develop good habits of desiring. We are speaking of an ideal that we should strive toward, not a state that must already be achieved. A true acceptance of our emotions will acknowledge our present bad habits—our pettiness, our lusts, our envy, and so on—but will also seek to change these habits. A true acceptance will acknowledge that these dispositions will be with us for a long time, for they generally do not disappear in a month, a year, or even ten years. But they do diminish, and with time new habits replace them. Aquinas is not burdening us with an unrealistic ideal. He is setting before us an ideal that is indeed challenging, but a true acceptance of our imperfections meets the challenge and moves forward.

Reasonable Emotions

Kant is right. We should do the right thing. But we should also desire rightly. Not only the will but the emotions as well are part of the moral life, for happiness is found in a well-ordered life. If human beings are distinctive in that they can understand the truth, including the truth of good and evil, then the emotions themselves should be elevated to the level of reason. As long as our emotions conflict with our sound judgments, with our deeper desires and our considered plans, then we will lack peace and harmony; our focus and energy will be distracted from the ultimate goal of our lives, and our happiness will be tarnished. Of course, it would be foolish to deny that much of the moral life is simply surging ahead, doing the right thing despite our emotions. While we know what is right, we often desire what is wrong. Much of the battle is realizing that these errant desires are not our true selves; they are merely passing emotions, not the solid foundation of reason and the will. Kant is right. The will is the most important part of the moral life. But it is not the sole part. By repeatedly choosing what is right, we not only solidify our resolution of will, but we also gradually modify our emotions, so that they begin to be shaped by reason.

7

Virtue and the Emotions

Anybody can become angry—that is easy. But to
be angry with the right person and to the right degree and
at the right time and for the right purpose, and in
the right way—that is not within everybody's
power and is not easy.

Aristotle

Knowing Is Not Doing

Ethics is sometimes presented as a series of complicated and difficult choices, for which we must become adept at sophisticated mental techniques. We are asked, "Is capital punishment justified?" "Should we legalize euthanasia?" "Is abortion morally wrong?" "Should we censor pornography?" Conflicting views are presented on these and other heated issues. Further, we are asked to comment on particular cases. Should Clare blow the whistle on her boss, who has cut some corners and broken some laws, even though she is likely to lose her job as a result? Should Michael be allowed to die from his throat cancer or should he be given a lethal injection? And so on. In the end, we are left with the impression that ethics is largely an intellectual endeavor, involving mental gymnastics of the most sophisticated sort that require hours of practice. If we can only straighten out the mess of conflicting values, then we will have done our ethics. The decisions will be reached and the choices made.

I don't want to belittle these questions as if they are insignificant. They have their place. But at best they are only half the story. They leave out much of the ethical life, for when the decision is reached, the choice is *not yet* made. Nor will it necessarily be made. After Anna decides that she should not embezzle money from her employer she has yet to choose. She might well choose to go ahead and embezzle. Knowing that embezzling is wrong is only half the battle. She must yet choose what is right. Indeed, knowing is the easy part; choosing is the challenge. Most embezzlers report that they knew they were doing wrong, but they did it anyway.

By focusing on conflicting opinions, contemporary ethics tends to obscure the role of our affective parts, of both our will and our emotions. It seems to say that we need only worry about sorting out differing values. We need not worry about choosing or about wanting; they will follow as a matter of course. Unfortunately, they will not. When I have determined that I should return the extra twenty, I do not automatically return it. I might well pocket it, especially since I long to have it. Figuring out what I should do is not the difficult matter. Doing it is. And doing follows upon choice, which is influenced by emotions. The true challenge of the moral life, then, is found in our desires, not in our thoughts. We need not strengthen our mental gymnastics so much as we must strengthen our inclination to good. We must develop those habits of desiring and choosing well.

The full story of ethics, then, must include an account of desiring well. That account is found in Aquinas's discussion of the virtues, for we desire well by way of the virtues. We are using "desire" in the broad sense, so that it covers the array of our diverse impulses to act. In this sense even anger is a desire; as we will see, we can have the emotion of anger for the right thing, in the right way, and at the right time.

We have all heard that patience is a virtue, but many other virtues do not receive the same publicity, for example, generosity, courage, moderation, justice, honesty, and humility. What do we mean when we say that patience, or generosity, or honesty, is a virtue? Certainly we are trying to say something good about patience; we are recommending it to others. A virtue, then, must be something good to have, but so are money and beauty, and these are not virtues, for neither money nor beauty indicates how a person behaves. In contrast, if someone is patient, then we know that he does not get irritable. Similarly, a generous person does not cling to his possessions but gives of them freely; an honest person speaks the truth; a courageous person faces dangers; in general, all virtues indicate some behavior that a person is inclined toward, for unlike money or beauty, virtue is a character trait. Since it is a *good* character trait, it disposes a person to good actions (I-II, 55). The opposite of virtue is vice, a bad character trait, such as irritability, greed, licentiousness, gluttony, arrogance, and cowardice.

Moderation

Moderation is a good place to begin understanding the virtues. Moderation or temperance is a virtue concerning the emotional desire for bodily pleasures (and the aversion of bodily pains). It especially concerns the pleasures of sex and food, for these are the two greatest bodily pleasures; other pleasures, says Aquinas, do not pose a sufficient temptation to merit a virtue (II-II, 141, 3 & 4). A person with moderation controls his desires for pleasure rather than letting these desires master him. He will desire those pleasures that are appropriate and flee those that are inappropriate. A married man, for instance, may well desire sexual relations with his wife, but he will be repulsed by the thought of sexual relations with another woman. Or again, a moderate person will desire those foods that reason recommends but not those that reason declares inappropriate.

What does moderation add beyond self-control? Recall that my friend has tempted me with ice cream. With my reason I have judged that I should abstain from the ice cream, but with my emotions I long to eat it. Let us suppose that in the end I resist the temptation, suggesting an alternate recreation to my friend. Have I acted moderately? It would seem so. I have controlled my desire for pleasure, not letting it get the better of me. As Kant would say, I have done the right thing; I have resisted the tug of inclination and have autonomously chosen to follow reason. Thomas would agree, yet he would insist that I do not have the virtue of moderation. I have acted rightly, but I have not yet attained virtue (II-II, 155, 1).

Virtue and Self-Control

Why not? What am I lacking? I have chosen rightly, but I have desired poorly. Although I *chose* not to eat the ice cream, nevertheless, I *wanted* to eat it. The moderate person would not only choose well; he would also desire well. Not only does his will follow reason; so do his emotions. In the above scenario, Aquinas would say that I am self-controlled but I am not moderate. I have an internal conflict between reason, which says I should not eat

79

the ice cream, and the emotions, which desire to eat it. I resolve this conflict with my choice, and since I side with reason rather than the emotions I am said to be self-controlled. If I side with the emotions, then I have lost control, and I am said to be weak-willed or one who loses control (II-II, 155; II-II, 156).

How does a moderate person differ from a self-controlled person? He lacks even an internal conflict. Reason says that he should not eat the ice cream, and his emotions follow. His emotions have been so habituated through past choices that they readily submit to the judgment of reason (II-II, 155, 1). When we say, then, that the moderate person controls his desires, we really mean it. He does not merely control his actions; he controls the desires themselves. He follows reason not only in his choices, but in his emotions as well. As we have seen in the last chapter, this sort of subjection of the emotions does not happen overnight; it develops through repeatedly controlling the emotions. A person is first of all self-controlled, and only with time does he become moderate.

Because the self-controlled person resolves his conflict through choice, self-control resides in the will (II-II, 155, 3). It is a disposition of the will to side with reason, even against the urgings of the emotions. In contrast, moderation is not only in the will. It implies a habit of following reason residing in the very emotions (I-II, 60, 2; I-II, 61, 2; I-II, 56, 4). The moderate person's emotions are more inclined to follow the judgment of reason than they are to follow the independent stirrings of the imagination (II-II, 155, 3, ad 1).

Which is better, self-control or moderation? A common attitude is that self-control is better than moderation. After all, the self-controlled person has resisted his temptation. He has fought a battle and won. In contrast, the moderate person has simply followed his desires, which were good from the beginning. What merit is there in that?

A whole lot: all the merit of having developed the habit of desiring well. The moderate person is not just lucky, as if his emotions are well-ordered by nature or by some God-given gift. Rather, through his own choices he has become moderate; his emotions have slowly come into line so that they now readily follow reason. Even apart from this merit—even if moderation were a gift from God (Thomas himself may have received such a gift)—Thomas would insist that moderation is better than self-control (I-II, 24, 3). The moderate person does not expend energy resisting his errant desires. He does not hesitate; he does not delay; he simply chooses well, because his disposition leads him to do so. His state, then, is the more perfect (I-II, 24, 3; II-II, 155, 4).

Sin and Imperfection

Most of us have not attained to this perfection; it does not follow that we are always sinning, for imperfection is not the same as sin. If a married man finds in himself an attraction to some other woman, then he is less than perfect, for his emotions are not conforming to the judgment of reason, which says that he should desire only his wife. Still, he might not be sinning. An errant desire is not necessarily a voluntary sin, for we readily acknowledge that our emotions arise spontaneously, apart from our choices. This married man, therefore, may not yet have sinned. The mere presence of his disordered desire does not make for sin. What matters is what he does with this desire. Does he dally with it, or even play with it, encourage it, begin to fantasize, or at the very least does he fail to check it? On the other hand, does he resist it, try to think of other things, and try to bring his desires in line with reason? Only if he takes the first approach does he sin voluntarily (I-II, 24, 1; I-II, 74, 3). The second approach involves imperfection but not sin. Indeed, imperfection is mixed with good: imperfection in the emotions but good in the strength of will to correct the emotions.

A married man (or woman), then, beyond understanding that he should be faithful, must also choose to be faithful. He must develop self-control, so that he can side with reason rather than with the emotions. Better yet, he must develop the virtue of moderation, so that even his emotions follow reason. Then he will truly have won the battle. Reaching the intellectual judgment to be faithful is the easy part. Actually remaining faithful is the true struggle of the ethical life.

What Is Vice?

We should also consider the state opposite to virtue, namely, vice. Aquinas follows Aristotle in saying that a virtue is always a mean between two vices, for we can fail from desiring well either by desiring too much or by desiring too little (I-II, 64, 1). With respect to bodily pleasure, of course, the almost universal human failing is to desire pleasures too much. When we think of a vice opposed to moderation, then, we think of gluttony (desiring the pleasures of food too much) or of lust (desiring the pleasures of sex too much). We ignore what Aquinas calls insensitivity (having insufficient desire of pleasures), because we aren't familiar with many people in this condition.

Yet consider that a married man might fail from moderate desires in two ways. He might desire another woman, and then he is desiring in excess, or he might, out of a puritanical attitude, not desire his own wife enough, and then he is failing by defect. The mean of virtue will correct both these failings.

Moderation, then, does not mean the absence of desire; it means the presence of appropriate desires. Moderation both spurs on desire and restrains it.

Just as self-control is a state halfway to virtue, so losing control is a state halfway to vice (II-II, 156, 3). The self-controlled person and the person who loses control share much in common (II-II, 155, 3). Their reason judges rightly about what is to be done; their emotions nevertheless desire what is wrong. Both, then, have an internal conflict between reason and desire. The two differ in the will, in the manner they resolve the conflict. While the self-controlled person chooses on the side of reason, the weak-willed person chooses on the side of the emotions.

Surprisingly, much is also shared by the virtuous person and the vicious person, by which I mean a person who has vice. The English word "vicious" has been debased to refer to someone who is cruel, but I am using it in its original sense, as the opposite of virtuous. Just as a virtuous person is someone with virtue, so a vicious person is someone with vice. At any rate, the two share much in common. For unlike self-control and weakness of will, both virtue and vice have no internal conflict between reason and the emotions. In the virtuous person, reason judges and the emotions follow. In the vicious person, the emotions desire and reason follows. Reason habitually capitulates to the longing of the emotions, for the vicious person has so habituated himself to his evil desires that he begins to perceive evil as good (II-II, 156, 3). The weak-willed person still retains his judgment; he chooses contrary to his judgment out of weakness rather than out of habit. But the vicious person chooses out of habit, so that his evil desires now appear good to him. He has that culpable ignorance of the true good that we discussed in chapter 4. He has abandoned his judgment telling him to pursue the good. He may know what in fact is good, but he no longer cares to pursue it. Both virtue and vice, then, express a unity of purpose. Beyond that, however, they could not be more opposed. Virtue sides with the true good perceived by reason; vice sides with the false good desired by the emotions.

The Spectrum of Character

If we imagine moral character as a continuum, ranging from the extreme of evil to the opposite extreme of perfection, then we find within it a fourfold division.[1] On the end of extreme evil we have the vicious person, in whom reason and the will habitually follow the errant desires of the passions. Next we have the weak-willed individual, who still retains the correct judgment of good and evil, but he does not often follow the judgment, for he sides with his desires. Next we have the self-controlled individual, who has errant desires but resists them. Finally, we have the virtuous person, who follows reason both in his choices and in his desires. This spectrum of character, however, is a continuum, so we should not suppose that the divisions are neat and precise. Someone might be more or less weak-willed, more or less vicious, and so on. Indeed, we can never really say that someone has arrived at virtue. Virtue is an ideal that we attain by degrees. We can always become better, strengthening yet more our inclination to the good.

We have seen this fourfold division applied to the virtue of moderation, but it might equally apply to many other virtues as well. Thomas is reluctant to apply the terms "weak-willed" or "self-controlled" to areas beyond the desire for pleasure, but the

---

1. A full listing may include more than these four, such as bestiality, or strong vice and pure vice, but this simplified division is sufficient for our purposes.

ideas may be transferred (II-II, 155, 2, ad 1). Regarding anger, for instance, someone might be in a state akin to self-control, getting angry in opposition to reason, but choosing in accord with reason (II-II, 156, 4). With regard to courage someone might be "weak-willed," for when reason says he should face a danger, he turns and runs, overcome by his emotion of fear.

Most of us, of course, are somewhere in the middle zones. We are neither particularly evil nor particularly good. We are weak-willed or self-controlled, but not yet vicious or virtuous. Still, we should not resign ourselves to this state. The moral life is largely a life of setting our desires in order. It is a lifelong project, never fully achieved, but immensely rewarding. Should a married woman be satisfied because she does not commit adultery, even though she is tempted to do so? No. She should root out the bad desires themselves. She should daily choose to control her desires. With time the control will become easier and easier, until it becomes second nature. The change will not come overnight, nor will it come by sitting back and waiting, but as it comes she will better love her husband and better choose what is right. Then she will have a true fidelity to her husband, for she will not even consider being unfaithful. She will have true peace of soul, having stilled her errant desires.

Some Other Virtues

Moderation is not the only virtue that concerns the regulation of our emotional life. To our diverse emotions correspond diverse virtues. While moderation is right desire concerning bodily pleasure, courage is right desire concerning fearing and daring. Similarly, patience is right desire concerning hardships, and generosity is right desire concerning wealth. For each distinct good desired by the emotions, says Aquinas, a distinct virtue regulates that desire (II-II, 114, 1). As we will see, yet other virtues concern reason and the will rather than the emotions, but for the moment let us consider some virtues of the emotions.

Courage or fortitude concerns dangers, and in particular the danger of death, so it addresses the emotions of daring and fear (II-II, 124, 3 & 4). A courageous person braves danger for the common good, but he also fears danger when facing it is pointless (II-II, 125, 1). A thief who braves the danger of robbing a bank, then, is not courageous. He braves a danger but not for the sake of the true good. He faces death or imprisonment in order that he might perform the evil action of theft (II-II, 125, 2, ad 2).

Courage is the mean between its two opposite vices, cowardice and foolhardiness (II-II, 125, 2; II-II, 127, 2).[2] When we say someone is not courageous, we most readily think of the coward, who fears what he should not, running from dangers that he should face; we do not usually think of a foolhardy person, for he puts on the appearance of courage. A foolhardy person dares even when he should not. The saying, "I dare you to ..." is meant to test a person's courage, but more often it only tests how foolish he is. Braving any danger whatsoever does not make a courageous person but a fool, for not every danger is worth facing. Each person, therefore, should examine himself to see whether he is more inclined to fear or to rashness, and then he should begin to pull his emotions in the opposite direction, so that he might thereby approach the mean of virtue. Of course, most of us fail on the side of cowardice rather than foolhardiness, so cowardice might be called the "natural" tendency of human beings.

2. Aquinas actually has three vices opposed to fortitude; he has not only cowardice and foolhardiness, but fearlessness as well (II-II, 126 &

Generosity is the virtue concerning the emotional desire for wealth, either in the form of money or in the form of possessions (II-II, 117, 3, especially ad 3). The opposite vice that readily comes to mind is greed, for a greedy person clings to his possessions, not wanting to share them with others, seeking to possess more and more, as if these things would make him happy (II-II, 118, 3). A generous person, on the other hand, will not be attached to his possessions, but will readily let go of them when the need arises (II-II, 117, 4). He will not seek more and more, but only what is necessary to maintain his state in life. He will not suppose that money makes him happy, but will recognize that money is merely useful. Opposite to greed, however, appears another vice, namely, a kind of prodigality or looseness with money (II-II, 119, 1). A prodigal person is so loose with his money that he cannot hold on to it. As a result he can never pay his bills, and eventually he may become broke. Like a greedy man, a prodigal person will seek more possessions than necessary. Unlike a greedy person he does not cling to these newly acquired possessions but uses them lavishly. In modern society we seem to suffer grievously from both vices. The escalation of individual debt arises both from a desire to possess many things and from a looseness with money that prevents someone from managing his affairs.

Which of these two vices, prodigality or greed, is the excess of desire and which is the defect? We readily suppose that greed is a kind of excessive desire for possessions. And so it is. Nevertheless, Aquinas places it on the side of defect. Why? Because the greatest challenge of generosity is sharing our possessions with others. While generosity also concerns a desire to acquire

---

127). The latter two are obviously closely related, so I have combined them into a single vice.

possessions, the virtue is itself defined by the more challenging aspect of sharing our possessions. For this reason, greed is a defect. As a desire to acquire possessions it is excessive; as a desire to share possessions it is defective. Prodigality, on the other hand, is an excess sharing.

The virtue of patience concerns hardships, so it focuses upon the emotion of sorrow (II-II, 136, 1). Our restrictive use of the word "patience," reserving the term almost exclusively for the hardship of waiting, is indicative of what we find important. Thomas, however, used "patience" to cover the proper endurance of any suffering. The telltale mark of a patient person is how well he bears hardships, for he does not give way to excessive sorrow. He stirs himself on to hope, that he might overcome his suffering. Besides excessive sorrow, finding its worst expression in self-pity, there is the opposite vice, a kind of insensitivity to one's own misfortune. Someone who does not sorrow over the death of a loved one is not patient, for he fails from the appropriate sorrow.

Closely related to patience is the regulation of anger, for sorrow often gives way to anger. Indeed, we perceive an impatient person as someone who readily gets angry. Aquinas, however, assigns the regulation of anger to the virtue of meekness (II-II, 157). The English word "meek" is hardly used today, outside of references to the beatitudes, so the word "patience" does duty for both of these virtues, at least when the anger is slight, what we would call irritation. The anger that Aquinas has in mind, however, goes well beyond irritation, and concerns the meting out of punishments; it might be described not merely as anger but as vengefulness. The meek person regulates this anger so that he is not excessive in his punishments. On the other hand, neither does he have the defect of remaining undisturbed by great evils that he should redress (II-II, 158, 2). A meek person will not blow up when someone cuts in front of him while driving, but he may get enraged when his employee is caught dipping his hand in the till. Given human nature, however, our anger is mostly inappropriate. If we wish to work at the virtue of patience, we will likely have to restrain our anger rather than encourage it. Still, our society does show a deep apathy toward some significant evils, such as abortion and pornography.

Humility is one of the most misunderstood virtues.[3] People suppose that a humble person is always cutting himself down, pointing out his own faults, and deprecating his merits, but such behavior is more likely to arise from false humility than from a true humility, which does not always debase oneself but rather is honest with oneself (II-II, 161, 1, ad 2). A humble person is justly praised for recognizing his own faults, something at which most of us are not very good, but he also recognizes his strengths (II-II, 132, 2, ad 1). A humble person knows himself and his position in the world. He does not seek to elevate himself higher than he ought, but neither does he sink himself lower. Most of us, however, have no problem with the latter; the former presents the continual struggle. Consequently, the humble person is known for what is most peculiar about him, his recognition of his own faults and limitations.

3. Once again I have simplified Aquinas. Regarding the achievement of excellence, Aquinas thinks we have two movements, one toward it (since it is a good thing) the other away from it (since it is difficult), and he has a virtue, with two corresponding vices, for each of these emotions (II-II, 161, 1). The virtue that regulates our movement away from high things is magnanimity (II-II, 129), a virtue taken from Aristotle that hardly has the appearance of virtue to the modern mind. The virtue that moderates our movement toward high things is humility (II-II, 161), which I have used for both virtues. The idea is that we must be careful not only to restrain our pride, but also to spur ourselves on toward great things.

Virtue	Concerning what object	Concerning what emotions	Vice of excess	Vice of deficiency
Moderation or temperance	Bodily pleasures	Desire	Intemperance	Has no name
Courage	Dangers	Braving and fearing	Foolhardiness	Cowardice
Generosity	Wealth	Desire to give or share wealth	Prodigality	Greed
Patience	Hardships	Sorrow	Self-pity	Has no name
Patience or meekness	Injustice done to oneself	Anger	Anger or impatience	Has no name
Humility	Excellence or accomplishments	Hope for excellence	Pride	Smallness of soul or false humility

Humility, says Thomas, is a virtue concerning our pursuit of great things (II-II, 129, 1 & 2; II-II, 131, 2; II-II, 132, 2). It finds the mean between elevating ourselves too high and debasing ourselves too low. Furthermore, the humble person does not dwell upon either his good points or his failings. He realizes his strengths; he realizes his weaknesses; and then he gets on with life, for he is not always thinking about himself. Consequently, he readily perceives other people's strengths. In contrast, a false humility puts on an outward show of humility, while inwardly the person craves for attention and recognition of his merits. He cuts himself down only in the hope that others will contradict him and praise his strengths (II-II, 161, 1, ad 2). He feels remorse for his faults only because he had imagined he was perfect. Furthermore, he is preoccupied with himself and rarely recognizes the good in others.

This modest sampling of virtues helps us to realize that the moral life is largely a matter of putting our emotional house in order, of straightening out our emotions and putting away our disordered desires. The task is not easy, but its accomplishment is replete with benefits. Every day of our lives we should all be working at one or two virtues. We should realize when our errant emotions arise, and we should bring them under the direction of reason. With perseverance, our desires will readily follow the lead of reason.

Virtue and Perception

The more our desires come in line, seeking the true good grasped by reason, the more will our perception of the good be certain and steady. When we discussed rationalizations we saw how errant desires might cloud our vision of what is truly good. Because we desire what is wrong, we try to dress up evil as if it were good. But if our emotions have been trained to follow the lead of reason, then rationalizations will become less and less common, for upon grasping the true good, we will then desire it. Our emotions will not oppose reason but support it.

We have also seen that the emotions affect our judgment of what is good, for reason perceives the satisfaction of the emotions as a kind of good. If I am angry at Bob, and only if I am angry at him, then it seems good to yell at him. Forming our emotions in the virtues, then, is important not only so that we follow the judgment of reason once made, but so that our reason judges properly in the first place, for well-ordered emotional desires will strengthen the judgment of reason, but disordered desires, which oppose the judgment of reason, will give rise to a contrary judgment. When the bank teller gives me an extra twenty, for instance, my reason says that I should return the money, but my emotions can affect that judgment in one of two ways. If I am generous and my desire for material possessions follows the judgment of reason, then I will not only judge that

I should return the twenty; I will also desire to return it. My original judgment will be strengthened by my desire, for returning the twenty will have the extra good quality of satisfying my desire. But if I am greedy, then in opposition to reason I will want to take the extra twenty. This errant desire will generate a contrary judgment. While I judge that returning the money is good, I will also judge that satisfying my greedy desire is good, so that it now seems good to take the money.

Aquinas approves of Aristotle's dictum that what appears good depends upon a person's disposition (I-II, 9, 2). To an irascible person, venting anger seems good; to a greedy person, accumulating wealth appears good; to a lustful person, sexual gratification appears good. It follows that if our emotions are in order, and we desire the true good, then what is truly good will also appear good to us, but if our emotions are disordered, stirred on toward imaginary goods in opposition to the judgment of reason, then what is in fact detrimental to our true well-being may appear good to us. To the distorted vision of an alcoholic, drinking to the point of inebriation appears good, even though it will only harm him physically and further ruin him spiritually. His judgment does not follow the truth of the matter; it follows his disposition, judging that the satisfaction of his desires is what matters most.

The more disordered our emotions become, the more will our judgment of the good be confused. Unfortunately, the depravity of human emotions seems to have no bounds. Some serial killers, for instance, seem to take sexual pleasure in killing people. Following Aristotle's dictum, then, we can say that to such people killing appears good, insofar as it satisfies their emotions.

Should we conclude that happiness for these people is found

in killing? Or should we conclude, rather, that their desires are misguided? They themselves will certainly judge that happiness is found in killing, for their judgment follows their desires. They do grasp a measure of truth, insofar as happiness involves the satisfaction of our desires. But ultimately their judgment is faulty, for these people are seeking satisfaction in what cannot fill the human heart. Not only are they seeking to gratify the emotions at the expense of the will, which seeks the fulfillment of our human capacities; even the emotion they seek to gratify will only lead to dissatisfaction.

Wealth cannot satisfy the human heart, but the greedy person is blind to this truth. His heart is set upon wealth, and his judgment follows his desire. He cannot imagine happiness in any other place than wealth. Nevertheless, the wealth he achieves never does satisfy him but only seems to aggravate his desire. Why? Because he can imagine wealth as satisfactory, but the reality, when he finally achieves it, does not match his imagination (I-II, 2, 1, ad 3). So he imagines yet more wealth, supposing it will satisfy, but the further wealth he acquires proves as fruitless as the first, and so he imagines yet more wealth. The more he has, the more he must puff up his goal for imaginary wealth, which he supposes will bring happiness. When dissatisfaction comes, he should conclude that he needs some other good besides wealth; instead, he concludes that he needs *more* wealth. Not only is he robbing himself of the enjoyment of the will, which finds peace in spiritual goods, but even his emotional desire for possessions is forever frustrated. Unfortunately, the more he pursues his misguided good, the more his desires become fixed upon it, and the more difficult it becomes to free himself from it; indeed, the greater his desire becomes, the more convinced he is that only wealth can satisfy.

His trouble is that he does not follow the judgment of reason, which seeks to determine what will truly fulfill the human potential. He follows the judgment of imagination, which has the capacity for the wildest fancies, far from the reality of the world around us. Human fulfillment is not realized in whatever we happen to imagine will satisfy us. It is found in truly human activity, including truly human desires, in desires that follow the judgment of reason.

Our faulty judgments of happiness, then, arise not only from misinformation; they also arise from our distorted desires. We seek to satisfy our desires, and if our desires are themselves misguided, then so too will be our judgment. We suppose that happiness will be found in acquiring whatever we happen to desire. In fact, happiness will be found in desiring the fulfillment of our human capacities. For our desires are themselves malleable. If we develop virtue, then even our emotions will be satisfied by the true good discovered by reason. But if we fall into vice, then even should we happen to achieve the true good it would not satisfy, for our desires themselves would be disfigured.

"What appears good depends upon our disposition." What lesson should we learn from this saying? That happiness is found in whatever we happen to desire? Such is the lesson that the vicious person takes. Rather, we should learn to conform our disposition to the true good. Virtue is important not only so that we desire rightly, but also so that we rightly perceive the good. If we do not guard our hearts carefully, then we doom ourselves to the pursuit of imaginary goods that provide only fleeting satisfaction.

Virtue and Habit

It should be clear by now that virtues are habits. We all have emotional dispositions of various sorts: some people get angry readily; others are easily excitable; still others are quick to rejoice in their own accomplishments. When these dispositions concern some moral good or evil, then they fall within the domain of virtue or vice, for virtues are good character traits and vices are bad character traits. Since character traits imply a disposition to behave in a certain way—in short, they describe our habits—a virtue is a habit by which we act well (I-II, 55). The virtues examined above concern the emotions; they are habits of desiring well. Moderation is that habit by which we desire bodily pleasures well. Generosity is that habit by which we desire material possessions well. And so on.

In each instance, "desiring well" refers to reason, for we perceive the true good and evil in things through reason. To desire well is to submit our emotions to the lead of reason; to desire poorly is to follow some impression of the imagination, without the vision provided by reason. In effect, desiring poorly is to become like a blind man who rejects his guide; not knowing the lay of the land, he will be led astray. By themselves the emotions are blind, for they do not perceive the true good and evil in things. Without reason to guide them, they will not hit upon the true good. Why should we desire blindly, when we can desire with vision? Why should we be led by impulses that have no understanding of the good, when we have a reason that can perceive the good and lead us to it? Why should we desire whatever strikes our fancy, when we could be desiring what is truly good? To abandon reason is foolishness. To follow reason is the wisdom of virtue.

The virtues that we have considered in this chapter all concern the emotions, but other virtues involve reason and the will, both of which can have their own habits. We should desire well in our emotions, but setting our emotional life in order is not enough. Our will must be strengthened in love and our reason must be well disposed in its grasp of the true good. In the next chapters, then, we will turn to virtues of the will and of reason.

8

Justice

*All men are by nature equal, made all of the
same earth by one Workman; and however we
deceive ourselves, as dear unto God is the poor
peasant as the mighty prince.*

Plato

Utilitarianism

The antithesis to the virtue of justice is probably realized in the
modern ethical theory called utilitarianism, as well as its many
offspring, which go by the name of consequentialism. For while
the virtue of justice seeks to treat others with equity and fair-
ness, utilitarianism disregards equality for the sake of quantity.
Utilitarianism was first advanced by the Englishman Jeremy
Bentham, who was twenty years Kant's junior. He described
the hedonistic calculus, a method of choosing between alterna-
tive actions by way of their effects. He said that whenever we are
faced with a decision we consider the effects of all our options,
and then choose that action that produces the most pleasurable

effects. For instance, if I must choose between watching a television show and reading Thomas Aquinas, then after I consider the effects of each, I will choose to read Aquinas, which gives me the greater pleasure. When this calculus is applied to laws concerning a whole people, and not just decisions about my individual actions, then the calculus must be broadened to include not only my pleasure, but the pleasure of everyone involved. The result, when applied to moral theory by later thinkers such as John Stuart Mill, is utilitarianism, which says that we must choose the action that produces the greatest pleasure for everyone involved. Suppose, for instance, that I must choose between reading Thomas and taking my nine-year-old daughter to soccer practice. While I would get more pleasure from staying home, my daughter would get more pleasure by going to practice. Furthermore, I also take some pleasure in watching my daughter. All told, then, I should take my daughter, for that will produce the greater happiness. Later forms of utilitarianism have seen many adaptations, most significantly a distancing from pleasure as the only good effect to be produced. Knowledge, friendship, health, and other good effects have been recommended as objects of pursuit. All these utilitarian views, however, hold in common the notion that we should act to produce the greatest number of goods (however defined) for the greatest amount of people.

The Injustice of Utilitarianism

We must acknowledge that utilitarianism has some truth. After all, we often choose actions based upon their effects, and we praise some laws because they bring great good to many people, while we condemn others because they bring about long-term harm. The effects of actions certainly have moral import (I-

II, 20, 5). The truth of utilitarianism, however, is limited, for it ignores some important features of our moral judgments. In particular, it doesn't take long to see how utilitarianism might often clash with justice. Consider dangerous medical experimentation, for which justice demands that we subject someone to danger only with his consent, usually because he himself gains something from the experiment. A cancer patient, for instance, might consent to an experimental form of chemotherapy because she has tried every other option. Although the experimental drug has its known and unknown dangers, she is willing to risk them for the possibility of recovery. But suppose a doctor gave her the drug without her consent? Would it be just? Worse yet, suppose a doctor surreptitiously performed a dangerous experiment that offered no potential benefit for the subjects. Clearly, he would have overstepped the bounds of justice. Just such experiments have been frighteningly frequent. The Nazi experiments upon the Jews are notorious, of course. Less well known are other cases, such as the radiation experiments performed by the United States military, in which patients were subjected to high doses of radiation in order to determine the level of radiation that would incapacitate someone. The patients themselves rarely received any benefit, and any consent they gave was questionable, as they were often not informed of possible risks such as cancer; they often belonged to minority populations, such as African Americans, or those considered socially useless, such as mentally retarded people or prisoners.

But what is a utilitarian to say to these experiments? They cause suffering for the patients, no doubt, but they also bring great benefit to society as a whole. We have learned much from the Nazi experiments as well as from the radiation experiments. It would be plausible to argue that while a few have suffered, many more have benefited. If perchance the benefits have not outweighed the harms in these cases, it would be easy to imagine more controlled experiments in which they would. On the face of it, then, utilitarianism reaches the conclusion that we can perform harmful, nonbeneficial experiments on patients, even without their consent, just so long as the experiments will produce more happiness for others.

Utilitarianism has proven as slippery as an eel, being nearly impossible to pin down to any definite conclusion. Indeed, utilitarianism seems to be a view that can reach any conclusion a person wants, if he is creative enough. Utilitarians, therefore, have attempted to slip out of the conclusion that we can perform harmful experiments for the benefit of others, citing such factors as long-term consequences of the policy, which might cause detrimental effects through patients' fear and mistrust. Be that as it may, the straightforward recommendation of utilitarianism is to pursue the experiments, and some utilitarians have been honest enough to bite the bullet and admit as much. At any rate, no matter how much utilitarianism might wind and slide and twist and turn, it cannot escape the conclusion that harmful experiments are justified if they produce a greater good for others. All their twisting can only avoid the conclusion that *this* particular experiment did produce greater happiness, or that *usually* such experiments produce greater happiness. Given their principles they cannot claim that abusing patients in this manner is inherently wrong.

Other examples of the conflict between utilitarianism and justice are easy to come by. It has been suggested that utilitarianism would condone framing an innocent person, if by so doing one could save the lives of many more. Furthermore, society might well benefit from a limited slavery, in which slavery for the few produces a greater happiness for the many. Or some have argued that our bodily parts might be open game for potential transplantation—even against our will and even while we are alive. After all, if we could dissect one individual, harvesting his heart, lungs, liver, kidneys, and other vital organs, we might be able to save the lives of five or ten others. Not a bad trade-off, in utilitarian terms. one life for five; the greater happiness is served.

But the virtue of justice would condemn these practices. We should never frame an innocent person, and we cannot kill an innocent person, even if by so doing we save many more. The sort of slavery in which a slave becomes a thing with no rights of his own is patently unjust. After all, justice is not concerned with producing good but with acting fairly. It is concerned with good actions, not with results; with the individual person, not with quantity.

Equality

The central feature of justice is equality (II-II, 57, 1 & 2; 58, 2 & 10); it treats each individual as an equal within the group. We have seen that utilitarianism might well treat one individual as a mere tool for the advancement of others' happiness. The individual comes to be treated as if his existence is a mere utility; he does not exist for his own good, but as an instrument for the promotion of some overriding good. The subject of an experiment, for example, is used to attain the good of useful knowledge. In contrast, justice treats no individual as the mere instrument for someone else's good; no individual exists simply for the sake of others. Each person is equal to the next.

Not, of course, that everyone is equally endowed. Common experience confirms that some people are more intelligent than others, some people are stronger, some are better at relating to others, and so on. We all have our natural gifts and capacities, and these gifts are not found equally in everyone. "Equal," then, must mean something else. Whatever our native capacities, we are all equally human and we are all equally members of the whole community. To treat another person as equal does not mean that they have the same capacities as we have; it means that they do not exist for us (I, 96, 4; I-II, 104, 1 ad 4). We must not be so far above others that their good is merely an instrument for our own. Rather, we are all on the same plane. No one's good is a goal for which others become instruments. Justice and utilitarianism, then, are polar opposites.

Thomas distinguishes between two kinds of equality, arithmetic equality and proportional equality, which correspond with two kinds of justice, commutative justice and distributive justice (II-II, 61, 1 & 2). Arithmetic equality, exemplified by a simple equation such as $2+3=5$, is illustrated in a simple exchange of goods. If I exchange my car for a new one, then I must also pay an additional sum to make up the difference, for my old car does not match the value of the new one. If the exchange is to be arithmetically equal, then I must supply something besides my used car, namely, cash.

This concept of equal exchange is understood by just about anyone, from children exchanging collector's cards to businessmen exchanging stock. It is a fundamental backbone of human intercourse. We seek a fair price for the items we buy, a fair wage for the work we provide, and a fair recompense for the house we sell. We are leery of shysters trying to rob us of our money and used car salesmen overcharging on a lemon. We instinctively know that human exchanges should be equal—arithmetically equal. Why? Because justice demands it. Because we are all equal, and no imbalance should be created through one person unfairly robbing another. Of course, there already exist monetary imbalances; some are rich and some are poor. That is not what is meant by equality, which guards not against a monetary imbalance, but against an imbalance of exchange, an imbalance of treating another person as a mere means to accumulate wealth. Injustice is found in our actions, not in some net result, as utilitarianism would have it.

Consider two ways someone might end up in destitute poverty. In one instance, he is swindled out of his possessions by crafty businessmen. In another instance, he loses all his possessions in a tornado that rips through town. Both have the same result, but only the first involves injustice. Certainly, the poverty resulting from the tornado is unfortunate—something we want to remedy with charity—but it is not unjust. Injustice involves exchanges between individuals. It involves treating others— through our actions—as unequals, as subordinates who exist for our own gain. In contrast, utilitarianism is concerned with the net result, and even then it is not concerned with equal results, but only with the accumulation of results.

From the central case of exchange of possessions commutative justice extends to other exchanges, or interactions, between individuals. Murder is unjust because it involves an unequal interaction, in which one person loses everything and the other nothing. No possessions are exchanged, but the good of life is lost through an "exchange" or interaction. Similarly, the "exchange" of talking about another person demands that we do no damage to the individual's reputation. In an extended sense, gratitude is something like justice; we return to others for what they have given to us.

The second sort of equality is proportionality, which is found not in exchanges between individuals—the equality of commutative justice—but in a group distributing rewards and punishments to its members—the equality of distributive justice. A business that gives merit raises, for instance, treats each person as an equal, but not by giving them arithmetically identical raises. Rather, the raises given are proportioned to the person's merit; more is given to an individual who has contributed more; less is given to him who contributed less. The resulting equality is proportional, like the equation $2/3 = 4/6$.

$$\frac{\text{raise of employee A}}{\substack{\text{previous contributions} \\ \text{of employee A}}} = \frac{\text{raise of employee B}}{\substack{\text{previous contributions} \\ \text{of employee B}}}$$

Although the numerical raises will differ from one another, the proportion of the raise to the merit will always be equal. Each person gets what he or she deserves. Aquinas notes that what counts for merit may differ from group to group, depending on what is considered important (II-II, 61, 2). Punishments also should be given in proportion to what the individual deserves. He who does a greater wrong should receive a greater punishment.

Just as we have seen that the arithmetic equality of commutative justice is fundamental to human intercourse, similarly, we find that everyone recognizes the justice of proportional distribution. Children complain when they are punished more, for an equal offense, than their siblings; workers complain when an incompetent peer is elevated to high levels; and a student complains when her paper gets a B even though it was just as good as someone else's paper that received an A. We all know that we should get what we deserve; unfortunately, we're best at seeking our own rewards and other people's punishments.

Equality, then, is the essence of justice. Not equality of end results, but equality of treatment. Each person must be treated as
an equal, as someone who is not subordinated to the good of others. We should not suppose, however, that the essence of justice
is found in individualism, that utilitarianism focuses upon the
group while justice focuses on the individual. The separation of
these two is a false dichotomy, for justice is concerned with the
individual person insofar as he is a member of a community.
Justice solely for an isolated individual makes no sense, for each
person belongs at least to the community of the human species.

Indeed, the good of the whole group takes precedence over
the good of the individual within the group (II-II, 64, 2; II-II, 58,
5). The net result, you might suppose, will look very much like
utilitarianism. For if the group is more important than the individual, then it seems that Thomas, like utilitarianism, will justify
doing harm to one individual in order to benefit the whole group.
But he does not. At least not as long as the individual is innocent.

He can avoid this conclusion because he operates with a different notion of a community than does utilitarianism. The utilitarian community is simply an aggregate, in which each member belongs to the whole as a certain quantity, as the bearer of so
much or so little happiness. In contrast, the virtue of justice is
founded upon an ordered community, in which each member belongs to the whole insofar as he fits within the order of the whole.
The difference is illustrated by comparing a pile of things to a machine. Both a pile and a machine are wholes composed of many
parts. But the parts of a pile merely contribute quantity, even as
each individual rock merely adds more mass to a mound of rocks.
In contrast the parts of a machine must be well ordered to one an-

other. Quantity alone is insufficient. Each part has some activity or function to play within the whole. If someone is making a pile of rocks, he might very well say, "The more the merrier," even as the utilitarian says the more happiness the better. But if someone is making a car, then he will not say, "The more wheels the better" or "More spark plugs are always better." No, a machine is not better because it has more parts. Rather, the parts are good only insofar as they contribute to the overall function of the machine.

A human community has four kinds of relations, the last three of which give rise to three distinct kinds of justice. First, the whole community is ordered to some good beyond itself, even as a medical community such as a hospital is ordered to healing. Second, each member must be ordered to the whole community, even as the health care professionals and other employees of a hospital must each contribute to the function of the hospital. Third, the whole community must relate to each individual, even as the hospital must pay its workers. Finally, each member must relate to other members, as one doctor will relate to another, or a doctor will relate to a nurse. The last three kinds of order give rise to legal justice, distributive justice, and commutative justice respectively (II-II, 58, 5; II-II, 61, 1).

We have already discussed commutative justice and distributive justice. We can now understand how they apply not only to individuals but to the community as well. In a well-ordered human community the members will be treated as equals. To the degree that the proper relations hold between individuals, to that degree the whole community will be directed to the ultimate goal. Put otherwise, in a well-functioning human community individuals are treated not as mere quantities but as persons directed to the good. After all, the common good resides most properly in the individual person (II-II, 64, 6).

Thomas does not say much about the third kind of justice, legal or political justice, the justice corresponding to the relation of the individual to the whole community. Its name arises from the role of law, which is to direct our activities to the common good (II-II, 58, 5), but it is perhaps better called political justice, to avoid the notion that this kind of justice merely concerns following human laws. According to Thomas, political justice is an overarching virtue, directing all other virtues. All that we do must be directed to the common good, for we are like parts of a whole, whose good arises from its order to the whole. It follows that all our actions must be directed by political justice, which immediately concerns the common good. Political justice, then, will direct all other virtues (II-II, 58, 6). The virtue of generosity, for instance, is ultimately regulated in terms of the common good, for I am generous with my money only insofar as I am using it for the good of the whole. Political justice directs but does not replace generosity, for my emotions still must be well disposed toward possessions.

Political justice has one particular aspect that may strike the modern mind as unusual. Justice directs us not only to other human beings but to God. God is not our equal; he is more like the community to whom we belong, for all that we do, and our very being, must be directed to him. Our good is truly good only insofar as it is a sharing in the divine good. As such, Aquinas thinks that a kind of natural religion is part of justice. This observation does not trespass into the boundaries of theology, which we said we would avoid at the beginning of this book. Aquinas is not claiming that he knows an obligation toward God by divine revelation; he is claiming that he knows this obligation by the light of natural reason.

Justice and the Good Life

The virtue of justice in all its forms seems to single out a truth most evident, which nevertheless our society is in danger of forgetting, namely, that the human good is not isolated but is had in union with others. The worst sort of calculated self-interest views all other human beings merely as tools and instruments for furthering our own good. At various times they can afford us pleasure, at other times we can get money from them, at still others they can provide assistance, and so on. Some people actually realize this anti-ideal, and while they may go far in the world, acquiring wealth and moving ahead of most people, their life is ultimately lonely. I do not mean that they are always alone, or even that they have no "friends." If they are affable enough they may even be well liked by many. Still, they are forever alone because they have no one with whom to share their lives. They have so conceived other people as tools that they cannot truly share themselves with anyone. To them no one is a person, an equal with whom they can share their lives; everyone is a servant, a slave, or even a thing.

Even though we human beings often make poor friends, we nevertheless have a deep-seated understanding that friendship is essential to our good. Whatever goods we accomplish are meaningless and pointless if we are utterly alone in the world, if we have no one with whom to share our accomplishments. If we take interest only in ourselves and not in others, then our good must be forever limited to ourselves. In contrast, if we take joy in others' good, then our good expands beyond our own lives into the lives of others.

The virtue of justice reflects the truth that human fulfillment is found in union with others. As the philosopher Aristotle says, by our very natures we are social animals, animals that are meant to achieve their perfection in community (*Politics* I, 2). The act of love, by which we seek the good of others, unites us to them. We all want to be loved by others; even more should we seek to love others, to unite our good with their good (II-II, 27, 1). If I attain the greatest mastery over my emotions, if I am accomplished in skills of many sorts, if I understand the mysteries of the universe, but if I have not love, then I am nothing. Whatever perfection I achieve, if it is just *my* perfection and not meant to be *our* perfection, then I have missed the ideal of human fulfillment.

The sharing of our human good is best realized in intimate friendship, for we cannot share our lives with every stranger in the street. Still, strangers are more than tools; each stranger is someone who can share in the human good. The virtue of justice simply says that we should treat everyone as an equal, as someone who can share in the human good, rather than merely as an instrument, as someone who might be useful in producing our private good. When we begin to use others as tools, harming them to achieve our own goals, then we are no longer attaining a truly human fulfillment. By isolating ourselves we are dooming ourselves to discontent, forever frustrating our natural propensity to be together with others.

A Virtue of the Will

Justice is a virtue not of the emotions but of the will (II-II, 58, 4). Moderation, courage, generosity, patience, and so on are all virtues that dispose our emotions to desire well. They primarily serve the purpose of reducing internal conflict, so that reason may think clearly and order our actions without opposition from the emotions. In contrast, justice is a virtue of the will. It concerns not our internal desires but our actions (I-II, 59, 4). Of course, even the virtues of the emotions concern actions indirectly, for our emotions propel us to act in various ways, but they chiefly concern the desires themselves (I-II, 60, 2). Because a moderate person desires sensible pleasures well, we are not likely to find him committing adultery; nevertheless, the virtue of moderation is not a virtue concerning acts of adultery, but a virtue concerning the desires for adultery. Justice, on the other hand, immediately concerns our actions, most particularly those actions that are directed toward other people (II-II, 58, 9).

Like the other virtues, justice is a habit, a fixed disposition of the will to seek what is just. It follows that a just man will not be fickle in his resolve for justice. He will not one day repay his debts and the next day steal from his neighbor. The single just act of repaying his debts does not make someone just, for such an act might arise from a whim or from outside pressure (such as fear of imprisonment). To be just, someone must have a steady disposition to act justly, day in and day out (II-II, 59, 2). It follows, too, that the just person will rejoice in acting justly. Suppose I return the extra twenty dollars that the bank teller has handed me. I have done the just thing; does it follow that I am just? Not necessarily. If I return the money only with great regrets, then I am not habitually disposed to act justly, for had I the habit of justice then acting justly would be spontaneous and pleasant.

Once again we see that the moral life is not just a matter of determining what is to be done and then doing it. Rather, the moral life is a lifetime project of developing the dispositions to act well. Justice is not merely doing the right thing; it is doing the right thing from a fixed disposition. We should not be surprised that becoming good takes effort and practice. Becoming good at golf is not merely a matter of discussing the best clubs to use in certain situations. Becoming good at painting doesn't follow from reading a few books on art. Why, then, should becoming a good person be just a matter of discussing ethical dilemmas? We need practice to become good in other areas; so too we need practice to become just. Only by our repeatedly acting justly will justice become second nature, something that we do easily and with pleasure. Of course, we develop the habit of justice only by first doing the right thing even when it is unpleasant. The virtue of justice, then, is attained by daily choosing to do what is right. We are what we do. Or at any rate, we become what we do. And that process of becoming is never-ending, as long as we walk on this earth. We must never cease the struggle to become yet more just.

9

Injustice

He who commits injustice is ever made more
wretched than he who suffers it.

Plato

Using Others

If justice is equality, then injustice is inequality, which is derived from the closely related word "iniquity." Injustice treats
others as tools, mere instruments for the sake of some further
good. The unjust person sets himself above others as the arbiter of their destinies. In this respect, the concept of injustice is
aptly expressed by Kant's second formulation of his categorical
imperative, a kind of overarching moral principle, which says
that we should always treat others as an end and never merely
as a means. Other people are not mere tools; their end and good
is not subordinate to ours. If Bob kills his aunt in order to come
into his inheritance, then clearly he is treating her as a mere
means to the end of wealth. Kant's categorical imperative would

condemn such abuse. We are all equals; the good of others is on par with our own. All injustice treats others as somehow subordinate—means to our own goals.

Thomas would not wholly endorse the categorical imperative, at least not without significant clarification. Kant wishes to treat everyone as an end because he thinks everyone is wholly autonomous, determining for himself the law he must follow. In other words, Kant is something of an individualist. One of Kant's formulations of the categorical imperative brings in a community, but it makes each individual a sovereign in a kingdom of ends.

Nevertheless, Aquinas could find much good in the second formulation of the categorical imperative, for the equality of justice implies that no single person's good stands above the rest, as the goal for which the others exist.[1] No one, therefore, is a mere means to someone else's good (I, 96, 4; I-II, 104, 1, ad 4). Nor can any single individual direct others to an end. We are "autonomous," in this sense, that we must direct ourselves to the end, but not in Kant's sense, that we determine the way to go. Rather than a kingdom of ends, in which each individual is an end unto himself, Thomas has a kingdom of individuals who direct themselves to one common end, the good of the whole human community. Everyone shares a common goal, rather than each individual being a separate goal, and for this reason we must treat everyone with love and respect.

No one, therefore, should treat another as a mere means, because doing so is opposed to the equality of justice. We have seen that justice has two equalities, giving rise to distributive and commutative justice; consequently, there will also be two

1. On the supernatural level, Christ would be an obvious exception.

kinds of inequity or injustice, one opposed to just distribution, the other opposed to justice between individuals.

Injustice of Distribution

The fundamental injustice of distribution is partiality; while it is commonly called "favoritism," it has been traditionally called "respect of persons," that is, treating someone in a special way apart from any merit on his part (II-II, 63, 1), as when a government official gives a coveted post not to the person who is qualified but to her best friend or to her daughter. The position is distributed not on the basis of merit but on the basis of some incidental quality. Similarly, a teacher who gives out grades based upon his likes and dislikes for certain students is playing favorites. Judges or juries oppose just distribution when they award plaintiffs based on sympathy rather than upon the justice of the cause, or when they give out too severe or too mild a punishment for the offense. In general, one opposes distributive justice by giving rewards and punishments apart from merit. Just distribution requires an equality of proportion, in which a person receives in proportion to his merit, so when someone receives either reward or punishment for some reason other than merit, injustice has been done.

Injustice of Exchange

Thomas spends more time on the injustices opposed to commutative justice. These include murder and lesser physical harms, theft, robbery, fraud, and usury, as well as harm inflicted through our words, through such things as backbiting, gossip, and perjury in court. We will consider each of these briefly.

Special attention should be given to the question of homicide, since in our age issues of life and death are hotly debated.

Some people claim that capital punishment is wrong, while others say it is just. Some people say that suicide and assisted suicide are good, while others claim that these are evil. Some people say that euthanasia is a bane; others that it is a boon. Thomas's teaching is rather simple and straightforward: killing an innocent person, even oneself, is never just, but society may sometimes justly put a criminal to death in capital punishment. The crucial distinction is between innocence and guilt. An innocent person still partakes of the common good, so he must never be killed. A guilty person, on the other hand, may be killed if he poses a great enough threat to society.

Such is the heart of Aquinas's teaching. Further explication will help us see the underlying rationale of his view. The injunction against killing another person falls under the more general precept that we should not inflict physical harm, of which killing is the most egregious form. We should not harm others because, as Kant would have it, by harming we treat others as a means. We treat them not as equals, but as subordinates, as things whose good is subservient to our own. Even if we persuade ourselves that we are, after all, only seeking our victim's own well-being, as the euthanizing doctor supposes that death is best for his victim, we are still placing ourselves above him, as a superior rather than as an equal, because we have arrogated for ourselves the role of judge, the one who can determine what is really good and useful.

But what if the person asks for it? What if he wants death? Many today would argue that such voluntary euthanasia, in which the patient asks to be killed, is acceptable and even desirable. Indeed, the voluntary nature of the act seems to remove some of the objections posed above. The doctor who merely fulfills his patient's request is not passing judgment upon his patient's good—

the patient himself has done that—nor does the doctor seem to be treating him as subservient. Indeed, Aquinas himself says that no one can suffer injustice willingly, for to suffer any harm is to endure what is contrary to one's will (II-II, 59, 3).

Nevertheless, Thomas would say that voluntary euthanasia is unjust. While the person might not be suffering an injustice, since the death is voluntary, nevertheless an injustice is being done. Justice requires that no innocent person ever be killed, because the innocent are the principal part of the common good (II-II, 64, 6). The argument presented here seems to refer to political justice rather than to commutative justice, for you will recall that political justice concerns an individual's relation to the common good. The idea seems to be that if we are really seeking the common good, as we all must, then we will not kill an innocent person, since he *constitutes* the common good. No individual can opt out of this common good by a mere will for self-destruction, for we as human beings exist not only for our own good but for the good of the whole. We cannot pick and choose our ultimate purpose; by our very makeup we are directed to the good of the whole human species. To reject this order is to offend against political justice.

For this reason Aquinas also rejects suicide (II-II, 64, 5). After all, voluntary euthanasia really is suicide; the individual has himself killed by another. If I hire a hit man, then I am a murderer, and if I hire a hit man to kill me, then I have committed suicide. At any rate, one objection Aquinas has against suicide is that it offends against the community. Why? Because the individual exists not simply for himself but for the good of the community. If a mother commits suicide then she has harmed not only herself, but her young children as well, and indeed the whole community. No one may rightfully reject this common good of political justice, so suicide and voluntary euthanasia will always be wrong.

Thomas does accept, however, the killing of criminals in capital punishment (II-II, 64, 2). The crucial factor is the criminal's guilt, for through his offense he has forfeited his share in the common good. He is no longer a constituent of the common good, but is an enemy of the common good. Human nature, says Aquinas, is changeable, by which he means that through our choices we can change the good to which we direct ourselves. A dog is fixed and determined in its ordination and can in no way move to any other good besides that designated by its nature. In contrast, we have the freedom to oppose the good for which we were made. We can pursue the common good, but we can attack it as well. When an individual does attack the common good and becomes a danger to it, then he may be cut off, even as a gangrened limb is cut from the whole body. Capital punishment was certainly more common in Aquinas's day than in our own, and for good reason, but Thomas leaves room for a legal system that has less need for capital punishment, for he says that human law sometimes allows a criminal to live so that he might repent of his offense, but if the criminal is too great a danger to society, then this time of repentance is not granted (II-II, 64, 2, ad 2).

Thomas also accepts killing in a just war. Again, some aspect of guilt is needed, for Aquinas says that the nation being attacked must be at fault. The war must set right some wrong; it cannot be simply for increased power or wealth. In World War II, for instance, when the allies went to war with Germany, Italy, and Japan, they sought to correct the unjust aggression of these countries. Aquinas gives other conditions of a just war besides the guilt of those attacked. The war must be declared by the appropriate authority, and those fighting for the just cause must seek to bring about good rather than evil. For our concerns, however, we need only note that even in war the killing of the innocent is never permissible.

Thomas also allows killing in self-defense, but his justification of it is too complex to address in this introduction (II-II, 64, 7). Let us say only that Thomas thought that some instances of self-defense were justified because the individual did not intend to kill; he merely intended to save his own life through actions that he realized might be lethal to his attacker.

In his explanation of lesser harms than killing, such as maiming or inflicting pain, Thomas lays the groundwork for informed consent. He says that removing a gangrened limb for the health of the whole body is legitimate, but only if the physician has the permission of the patient, or if the care of the patient has been given over to the physician (thereby leaving room for an implied consent or a proxy consent) (II-II, 65, 1). As we have already seen, this requirement of consent arises from the equality between individuals. The doctor cannot place himself above his patient, as the arbiter of his good, without undermining the equality that should exist between everyone.

Theft and Robbery

Theft and robbery harm an individual not in his person but in his possessions (II-II, 66, 6). Theft is the secret or surreptitious taking of property (II-II, 66, 3); robbery is taking property with the use of force, such as a mugging (II-II, 66, 4). Once again, these unjust actions offend against the equality due to others. They may not strictly count as *using* another person, since the possessions are used rather than the person; nevertheless, the victim is not treated as someone whose good—including the good of his possessions—is of equal worth with the offender's. His good is treated as subordinate to the perpetrator's, who deems his own good as the end for which others may be used.

Since private property involves the convention of ownership, Aquinas allows a little leeway for the taking of property; he grants that in necessity someone may take what belongs to another (II-II, 66, 7). Well, not quite. Rather, in necessity the human convention of ownership breaks down, for no one can claim to own what is necessary for another. Someone who is starving can take a piece of bread; I can take your boat if I need it to save a drowning woman, and so on. No doubt these cases of necessity are rare, but we cannot possibly foresee all the situations where they might arise. The idea is that possessions were given for the human good. Furthermore, this good requires that we distribute possessions according to ownership, for human society could not function without each person caring for that which belongs to him (II-II, 66, 2). Still, this convention of ownership cannot override the first purpose of possessions, which is for the human good. Therefore, in necessity, the legal possession breaks down and ownership becomes common.

Injustice through Speech

Aquinas spends more time on offenses of speech than he does on any other injustice, in part because we can harm others through our speech in a plethora of ways. He divides injustice of speech into two broad categories, those involved in the courtroom and those outside the courtroom.

The classic courtroom offense is perjury. To falsely accuse someone of a crime, or to falsely testify against someone, is an egregious offense indeed (II-II, 70, 4). You can ruin a person's whole life, perhaps sending him to prison or even to death. The offenses outside the courtroom, however, are far more common. Indeed, they are nearly daily occurrences in most people's lives. Consider how often we gossip, backbite, and so on. Yet these are serious offenses, more serious even than theft or robbery, for they destroy someone's reputation, a more precious good than mere material possessions (II-II, 73, 3); "sticks and stones may break my bones but words will never hurt me" is not quite true.

Injustice Is a Habit

We have discussed several unjust actions, such as murder, theft, and perjury, but we cannot leave the topic of injustice without noting that injustice, like justice, is a habit. Someone is unjust not simply if he performs an unjust action, but only if he acts unjustly from the habit of injustice (II-II, 59, 2). If I finally decide to pocket the extra twenty dollars, then I have committed an unjust action. Am I thereby unjust? Not necessarily. My action might have arisen from the passion of the moment rather than from a steady habit of choosing injustice. Injustice is a vice; it is not mere wrongdoing. If virtue is the ideal of spontaneously and joyfully doing what is just, then vice is the anti-ideal of someone who spontaneously does injustice and relishes it. Like the habit of justice, the habit of injustice resides in the will, by which we choose to act. It is not simply a regular emotional desire; it is a steady disposition of the will. When someone has come to this state he is far gone indeed; retrieving him, so that he once again loves the true good, may be nearly impossible, at least apart from divine help.

The moral life is not simply a matter of knowing the rules but a lifetime project of developing the proper dispositions. So too, is the immoral life. We often suppose that our individual choices are only that, single isolated choices. But they are not.

They are bound by habit to our past choices, and they influence our future choices. As we do an evil deed, we tell ourselves, "Just this once," as if we could isolate this choice from the rest of our lives. But when we do wrong we start down a path, and the further down that path we travel, the more difficult it becomes to turn around. Habits cannot be undone in a day.

Do we really want to become the person that our choices are leading us to? By repeatedly raising ourselves above others, do we want to end up arrogant? By harsh ambition, do we wish to become cold and heartless? By lazy indifference, do we wish to become a burdensome slouch? By always thinking of our own advantage, do we wish to become a selfish Scrooge? Such personalities are unpleasant, even repugnant. But they do not arise inexplicably from nowhere. They come from individual actions, the sorts of actions that we often make during our days.

Plato has Thrasymachus suggest that the perfectly unjust man leads a happy life. If we imagine that happiness is found in worldly success and wealth, then he has a case, for cheaters and thieves often get ahead in the world. The very word "politician" is almost synonymous with corruption. But we must ask whether such "happiness" is worth it. Would we really want to be a Hitler, if that's what it took to be successful? Would we wish to be a wealthy Ebenezer Scrooge or rather a poor Bob Cratchit? Happiness, it may turn out, has much more to do with who we are than with what we have.

As we have seen, twisted personalities bring with them a distorted vision of the good life. The further we walk down the path of injustice, the more clouded becomes our understanding of happiness. If we now stand above the valley of injustice, so that with a clear vision and perspective, we can see that being selfish, ambitious, or cruel is repugnant, then we should be careful to guard our outlook. Each unjust action we perform is a step down into the valley. While each step is small and simple in itself, we will find with time that turning around becomes an overwhelming burden. All the while our perspective itself changes, so that we no longer perceive that our own arrogance and selfishness are distasteful.

Can we ever persuade unjust people that they have taken the wrong path, that they have taken the road of discontent rather than the way of joy? Probably not. Their vision has become so clouded that they suppose the perspectives of generous and kind people are all fanciful myths. Perhaps they pride themselves for recognizing the harsh realities of life, and they scoff at virtue as sentimentality. Such as these refuse even to look toward the light; to them the truth will remain forever hidden.

IO

Intrinsically Evil Actions

Some actions and emotions ... imply by their very
names that they are bad.... It is, therefore, impossible
ever to do right in performing them: to perform them
is always to do wrong. In cases of this sort, let us say
adultery, rightness and wrongness do not depend on
committing it with the right woman at the right time
and in the right manner, but simply committing
such actions at all is to do wrong.

Aristotle

Actions Wrong in Themselves

Utilitarianism denies that any actions are universally wrong, no matter the circumstances. Take killing the innocent, for instance. Many people, Thomas included, would say we must never kill an innocent human being. No matter the circumstances, no matter the dire consequences that might follow from not killing, and no matter the noble motives of the killer, murder is always wrong everywhere and at all times. Utilitarianism, however, would disagree. After all, sometimes killing an innocent person might bring about more good for others.

A classic example involves a man, let us call him Bernard, who happens upon a dictator ready to have twenty innocent people killed. Bernard protests the action, but the dictator does not listen. Finally, he relents, saying that he will not kill the twenty, just so long as Bernard kills one of them. Now Aquinas would insist that we should never kill an innocent person. On the other hand, a utilitarian would point out that by killing one person Bernard is bringing about a much greater good, for he is saving nineteen. We have already seen, as well, the example of framing an innocent person—which Aquinas would consider wrong in all situations at all times—in order to save many others. Utilitarianism justifies these sorts of actions, but Aquinas does not.

While Aquinas did not actually confront utilitarianism in his lifetime, he did encounter similar sorts of situational ethics. In the century before Aquinas, for instance, Peter Abelard had defended an ethics of good intentions. An action is good or evil, he insisted, depending upon a person's intention. His view was not so simplistic as to justify any action just so long as it arose from a good intention, but he did say that the act itself did not have moral worth apart from the person's intention. Similar views retain their appeal today. All that matters, we are told, is that we act lovingly; our individual actions are not so crucial as is our fundamental disposition. These views are appealing because they allow us to justify almost anything we want badly enough. We can usually fabricate good intentions for our selfish actions.

Abelard was particularly adept at coming up with interesting examples. Suppose a man sleeps with a woman who is not his wife—an act of adultery—but he mistakenly thinks that she is his wife. Then we surely would not blame him—he would not have sinned—so the act of sleeping with another woman cannot itself be wrong, apart from intention. As unlikely and humorous as this example is, it seems to be taken from the scriptural account of Jacob and Leah, who was not the woman Jacob supposed he was marrying (Rachel). Similarly, rape is not sinful for the woman raped, for she does not consent to the act. Once again, it seems that the act itself is not evil. Or, suggests Abelard in a twist upon *Oedipus Rex,* a man might marry his own sister—an act of incest—but be unaware that she is his sister. Since he would be free of guilt, it follows that the act of marrying one's sister cannot be wrong of itself. Or consider two executioners putting to death two criminals. One does so out of a love of justice, the other out of revenge. The first one has not sinned, while the second has. Therefore, intention determines the evil, not the nature of the action itself.

Human Actions

Except for the last example (concerning which Aquinas agrees with Abelard; see I-II, 1, 3, ad 3), all of these cases involve a failure to appreciate the nature of human actions, for Abelard's examples do not involve human acts, but what Aquinas calls acts of a human being. According to Aquinas, a human act is a voluntary and deliberate action (I-II, 1, 1). Driving a car, eating breakfast, and reading a book are all (usually) human acts. On the other hand, rolling over in one's sleep, unconsciously rubbing one's beard, and tripping and falling are not human acts. We do not voluntarily roll over in our sleep, and we do not try to trip and fall. These actions Aquinas does not call human actions, but acts of a human being. They are actions performed *by* a human being, for *I* roll over, *I* scratch, and *I* trip. Nevertheless, these actions are not done insofar as I am human.

The idea is that we act *as human beings* when we act from our peculiarly human capacities of reason and will. My heart pumps, my hair grows, and my body falls under the weight of gravity. All of these are things that my body does; they are not, however, things that I do as human. They do not arise from what makes me to be human. My heart pumps and my hair grows simply because I am a mammal; I fall under the force of gravity merely because I am a body. Only if I act from reason and will, deliberately and voluntarily, do I perform a truly human action, an action that arises from me as a human being. As the philosopher Ralph McInerny has put it, a golfer may do many things, from buying a car to hitting a hole in one, but what he does *as a golfer* is to golf.[1] A dancer is not limited to dancing, but what she does *as a dancer* is to dance. Similarly, human beings do many things, from rolling over in their sleep to reading newspapers, but what they do *as human beings* must be deliberate and voluntary.

What does all this have to do with Abelard? Well, the man who mistakenly sleeps with another woman, the victim of rape, and the man ignorant of his incest all perform actions that are not wholly human; they lack some element of deliberation and will. The rape victim is the clearest case, for she in no way chooses her action. Her action is not human, and then neither is it moral; it is something that happens to her, not something she does. The other cases are less clear. The man who sleeps with another woman, thinking she is his wife, for instance, has performed the bodily activity that we would describe as "sleeping with another woman," but he has not performed the human action of "sleeping with another woman," for the act that he chose to perform was "sleeping with his wife."

1. Ralph McInerny, *Aquinas on Human Action: A Theory of Practice* (Washington, D.C.: The Catholic University of America Press, 1992), 3–24.

When you hear that Bruce has killed Paula, you are horrified. But then you discover that Bruce fell from a three-story window and landed upon Paula, thereby killing her; you are no longer so appalled by Bruce's behavior. Indeed, Bruce never really performed the *behavior* of killing. His body killed Paula, but he did not. When we first hear that Bruce has killed Paula, we assume that it was a human action, an intentional act on Bruce's part to end the life of Paula. But when we discover the truth of the matter we realize that Bruce has "killed" Paula only in an extended sense of the word "kill." He did not perform the human action of killing. Rather, his body went through a process that resulted in Paula's death.

It would be absurd to say, "Having sexual relations outside of marriage is sometimes okay for a woman, as when she is raped, and sometimes not okay, as when the woman consents to it." Being raped and consenting to sexual relations do not belong to the same sort of action. They are the same physical process, but they are disparate as human actions. Being raped does not even fall in the moral ballpark, for it is not a human action. We do not morally appraise someone for having good or bad digestion, for the physical process of digestion is not a human action. No more, then, do we morally appraise someone for being forced into sexual activity, for the coerced physical process of sex is not a human action. It does not show up on the moral radar screen.

What, then, of the man who sleeps with another woman, thinking her to be his wife? This case is not so straightforward. The man certainly does something voluntary: he does sleep with a woman. At the same time, however, he has not performed the human action of sleeping *with another woman* any more than Bruce performed the human act of killing Paula. What the man did, as a human action, was to sleep with his wife, for a human action arises from our deliberation and will; what he deliberated about and what he willed to do was to sleep with his wife. The physical process that resulted, however, was an act of sleeping with another woman. But this "action" is better described as an act of a human being, not as a human action. As such, it does not fall in the moral ballpark. A similar point can be made of the man who unwittingly marries his sister.

It is unfair, then, to say that the action "sleeping with another woman" is sometimes evil, when the man is aware of it, and sometime good, when he is unaware, thereby concluding that the morality of an action depends upon someone's intention. For "sleeping with another woman" can mean two different things. When done with knowledge, it is a human action; when done in ignorance, it is an act of a human being. The two happen to have the same verbal description, they involve the same physical processes, but the actions are entirely distinct.

The Act Itself

What should we say, then, of sleeping with another woman? Is the action evil of itself or is it evil only through the person's intention? We can say, at least, that Abelard's objections do not settle the matter. He does not compare two apples and find that one is rotten and the other good; rather, he compares an apple and an orange. If he were really to focus upon two apples—two instances of the human act of sleeping with another woman—then Abelard himself would not grant that one of the two could be evil and the other good; rather, we may suppose that he would agree with the judgment of his day, that such an act is always evil.

Some modern theologians claiming to follow Aquinas, however, have no such scruples. They are eager to grant that sleeping with another woman, even knowingly, can sometimes be good. In short, adultery is not always evil. In so saying, these theologians depart from the teaching of Aquinas, who taught that some acts are evil in themselves, adultery included, no matter the circumstances or motive of the one acting.

Aquinas's case depends upon a distinction between an action and its circumstances, including the most important circumstance of all, the agent's motive. For example, if Colonel Mustard murders Miss Scarlett, then the act itself would be murder. That it is done in the study, at midnight, and with the candlestick, would all be circumstances. In total Thomas lists eight different kinds of circumstances (I-II, 7, 3). We have already indicated (1) place, (2) time, and (3) with what instrument or aid. In addition, there are (4) who did it (Colonel Mustard), (5) why he did it, that is, the motive, (6) how it was done (quickly, carelessly, etc.), (7) the effects, and (8) that upon which the action was done (such as Miss Scarlet). In an act of euthanasia, for instance, we can identify the act itself as killing an innocent human being. The circumstances would include the following (1) it was done in a hospital, (2) at 3:00 P.M., (3) with an injection of morphine, (4) by a doctor, (5) for the sake of ending the person's misery, (6) quickly, (7) with several effects, including the following: the victim's wife inherited one million dollars, a bed was freed for another patient, the victim's daughter went into depression, and so on, and finally (8) the action was performed upon a terminally ill individual.

Some people would claim that you cannot evaluate an action morally unless you consider all the circumstances, a task that would seem endless, especially given the multiplicity of effects and aspects of the thing acted upon. The terminally ill patient, for instance, is also six feet five inches, balding, is a member of a chess club, and so on. Must we consider all these circumstances before we can make a moral evaluation of the action? It would seem not. Rather, we can sometimes determine the good or evil of an action independently of its circumstances. Bernard's act of killing the innocent man, for instance, is evil despite his good motive (of wishing to save others) and despite the good effects (of actually saving others), for the very act of killing an innocent human being is evil in all circumstances.

Action, Circumstance, and Motive

When we evaluate an action morally, we must consider three factors: the action itself, the circumstances, and the agent's motive (set apart as the morally most significant circumstance) (I-II, 18, 2-4). By their very nature, apart from circumstances, some actions are good while others are evil (I-II, 18, 2). The action of feeding the hungry, for instance, is good by its very nature; in contrast, the act of having sexual relations with another's spouse is evil by its very nature. Besides good and evil actions, we might add a third moral category, namely, indifferent actions (I-II, 18, 8). The act of picking up sticks, for instance, is of itself neither good nor evil. We will see, however, that this third category must be clarified.

The circumstances affect the morality of an action in two distinct ways. First, a circumstance might affect the degree of good or evil (I-II, 18, 11). For instance, the act of taking what belongs to another (theft) is evil of itself, but the degree of evil might depend upon a variety of circumstances. Did the thief take five thousand dollars or merely fifty dollars? The former is much worse than the latter, therefore, this circumstance of how much (an aspect of that about which the action is performed) affects the degree of evil. Similarly, "to whom the money belongs" (another aspect of that about which) might affect the degree of evil: was it a millionaire or a pauper? Although it is not right to take fifty dollars even from a millionaire, nevertheless, it is not so bad as taking the same amount from a pauper. Circumstances can also affect the degree of good found in an action. The act of giving alms to the poor, for instance, is good in itself, but the poor widow's mite is better than the billionaire's multimillion-dollar contribution. Why? Because the circumstance of who is giving affects the degree of good. Or again, if two people with equal circumstances and incomes were to give five hundred dollars and one thousand dollars, the gift of one thousand dollars would be better.

Circumstances can also affect the morality of an action by taking what was a good or indifferent action and transforming it into an evil action (I-II, 18, 10). Consider, for example, that the marital act is by its nature good. But if that action is performed in a public place (the circumstance of where), then it becomes an evil action of exhibition. Similarly, the indifferent act of spitting becomes sacrilege if one spits upon an altar (the circumstance of that upon which or of where). Furthermore, a circumstance might transform an already evil action into yet another kind of evil. The act of theft, for instance, is evil in itself, but another evil is added if the object stolen (circumstance about which) is a holy object, for then it becomes sacrilege.

A circumstance can certainly transform an indifferent action into a good action; no circumstance, however, can make an evil action to be good (I-II, 18, 4, ad 3). Robin Hood's deeds, for instance, cannot be justified. The act of robbery, which is already evil in itself, cannot be made good through the motive of wishing to give the money to the poor. Nor can Bernard's action be justified. Killing an innocent human being is evil in itself, and the good effect (of saving more lives) does not make it to be good.

Why is there this asymmetry, such that good actions can become evil but evil actions cannot become good? Because, says Thomas, good requires that everything be in place while evil follows if only one essential thing is out of place (I-II, 88, 6, ad 3; I-II, 20, 2; II-II, 110, 3). A good action must have everything in order—the act itself, the motive, and all the circumstances—but an action is evil if only one of these is defective. Similarly, a car is good only if all of its essential features are in order, but it is bad if only one feature is lacking. You would hardly be impressed were I to sell you a car that was missing a radiator, insisting that the car is really good, since only one thing is missing. Similarly, an action is not good if only one essential factor is out of place.

The final element of the triad, the motive or goal for which the action is performed, is simply the morally most significant circumstance. A bad motive can vitiate any good or indifferent action. If I give to the poor only because I want others to praise me, then the action is no longer good. If I pick up sticks in order to signal to an undercover agent to blow up the embassy, then my action has become evil. Furthermore, a good motive can make an indifferent action good, as when I pick up sticks in order to help someone clean her yard. But once again, a good motive does not make an evil action good. As is commonly said, a good end does not justify an evil means. Once the action is evil it remains evil, regardless of the agent's good intentions.

Action, circumstance, and motive, then, determine the morality of an action. The act itself may be good, evil, or indifferent. The circumstances affect the degree of good or evil, or they may transform a previously good action to evil or take an indifferent action and make it either good or evil. They may not, however, take an evil action and make it good. The end or motive plays a similar role.

Indifferent Actions

We must qualify our statement that actions may be either good, evil, or indifferent, for when Aquinas asks whether any human actions are morally indifferent he answers, "Yes and no." Yes, some actions, such as picking up sticks, are morally indifferent. On the other hand, no action of picking up sticks is morally indifferent; all such acts are either good or evil. What does Aquinas mean? He means that the action of picking up sticks, considered in general, has neither good nor evil necessarily attached to it (I-II, 18, 8). Good or evil, however, may come to it through some circumstance or end, as we have already indicated. If I pick up sticks with the intention of throwing them at an innocent bystander, then my evil motive vitiates the action. In the concrete situation the indifferent act of picking up sticks has taken on the character of evil. Or if I pick up sticks in order to tidy up a bedridden woman's yard, then what was indifferent has taken on the character of a good action.

We must distinguish, therefore, between "picking up sticks" considered by itself, and "picking up sticks" as it exists in the concrete situation. In the first sense, it is indifferent; in the second it may become good or evil. Indeed, Aquinas goes so far as to say, that in the second sense, it *must* become good or evil (I-II, 18, 9). It cannot remain indifferent. Some circumstance—especially the motive—will inevitably give moral character to the concrete action. Why? Because whenever we act, we act for some good, and that good must itself be a true moral good, fitting for the action, or only an apparent good. Whenever we pick up sticks, then, we do so for some true good or for some deficient good, which we would like to think good. It follows that the concrete act of picking up sticks must be either good or evil.

A further clarification can be made. Sometimes simple acts like picking up a stick or scratching one's beard can be involuntary; they arise absentmindedly, without deliberation, by a kind of impulse arising from the imagination, without the intervention of deliberating reason. Such actions are not indifferent, nor do they become good or evil in the concrete. Rather, they are, as we have seen, acts of a human being, which do not even enter the moral ballpark. They have no moral designation whatsoever. The indifferent acts that Aquinas considers are human actions, deliberate actions done for some reason; as such, they will be good or evil in the concrete.

Where Did Abelard Go?

What, then, are we to say about sleeping with another woman? What are we to say about Bernard killing one innocent person in the hopes of saving nineteen others? We must say that neither of these actions can be justified. Both are intrinsically evil actions, actions evil by their nature, regardless of any circumstance. The addition of circumstances can never take what is inherently defective and make it whole. These actions are already evil from their objects, and cannot be made good by intention or circumstance.

Not only murder and adultery are actions evil by their nature. Fornication, rape, homosexual behavior, theft, robbery, backbiting, lying, blasphemy, and others are also evil in every circumstance. Some of these examples demand further reflection upon their content, but when the reflection is complete their universal prohibition must be upheld. Theft, for instance, refers to taking what belongs to another, which Aquinas says is wrong in every situation (II-II, 66, 5). On the other hand, he says that in necessity someone can take what is needed, as a starving man might take a loaf of bread. How are these two statements to be reconciled? By realizing that possession is not entirely determined by human legal systems. Although human laws operate for the most part to determine that, for instance, my car belongs to me and not to you, they break down in unusual circumstances, which cannot be foreseen by a general human law. In necessity, says Aquinas, all things are held in common (II-II, 66, 7). Similarly, clarifications could be made about lying. While lying is never right, hiding the truth can sometimes be acceptable; one may even dissimulate in order to hide the truth, that is, without lying one might distract someone from the truth (II-II, 110, 3, ad 4).

Special mention should be made of Abelard's two executioners. Both kill a criminal deserving of death, but one does so for the sake of justice while the other acts from personal revenge. Thomas agrees with Abelard's judgment: the act of the first executioner is good but the act of the second is evil. Aquinas, however, can provide a better account of the good and evil. The action considered in itself is good, but the motive of each executioner further affects the good or evil of the act. The evil motive of the second executioner takes what was a good act and makes it to be evil.

Ultimately, Thomas rejects the situational ethics that would leave everything up to circumstances. No doubt circumstances and situations are important. No doubt ethics has its gray areas. It does not follow that circumstances are everything. It does not follow that nothing is black and white. Moral decisions do require a consideration of the circumstances and motive. Nevertheless, we know that some actions are wrong no matter the circumstances. We should not become so overawed by the gray areas of life that we forget the black and white.

II

Virtue and Truth

❦

All men by nature desire to know.
Aristotle

The unexamined life is not worth living.
Socrates, in Plato's apology

Intellectual Virtues

Ethics does not tell us the truths of science; it does not teach us mathematics or physics; nor does it teach us how to be a doctor or an architect. We might be surprised to find, then, that Aquinas lists science as a virtue, and that various skills, such as medicine or architecture, also count as virtues (I-II, 57). Our surprise may be dispelled when we remember that ethics does not so much concern rules of right and wrong as it concerns guidelines of how to lead a good life. A truly fulfilling human life will realize our human capacities, especially those associated with reason. We are distinct from all other animals in that we can reason; we alone can understand the world around us.

Should not our fulfillment, then, include the development of our minds? And since ethics concerns our fulfillment, then should not the development of our minds, as well as our hearts, be counted as virtue?

If we are to lead a human life, and not merely an animal life, then we should understand the world around us. Animals certainly have some sort of knowledge—they have sensation and memory and a bit of instinctive know-how—but ultimately they do not understand the things around them. They do not know the causes of things, as we do through our studies of science; they do not grasp the natures of things, nor do they do mathematics or ask philosophical questions. Our minds far surpass the animals'. A fulfilling human life, then, must develop this unique mind.

We are not satisfied with mere sensation or mere memory, since we have the ability to grasp the reasons for things. This need to get beyond sensation is reflected even in our appreciation of sensible beauty. The beauty of a symphony is not found simply in certain pleasant sounds, but in the order and structure of those sounds, which is grasped by reason. Animals have no artistic appreciation, even if they are pleased by the sounds of music, for they don't grasp the order of the whole. Similarly, the beauty of a painting rests upon an order of the parts.

Indeed, our enjoyment of science or of philosophy can also be somewhat aesthetic, for by understanding the interrelation of the many causes in the universe we come to perceive a magnificent order, unified into a beautiful composition (II-II, 180, 2, ad 3). Who can look at the wonder of the genetic code without seeing its beauty, or who can fail to grasp the beauty behind the workings of the solar system? Indeed, Einstein suggested that the general theory of relativity is recommended by the sheer beauty of its mathematics. This beauty of science is more wholly intellectual than is the beauty of sensation, but in either event the mind is engaged.

Human reason is also involved in the fulfillment we find in certain skills. The accomplishment of becoming a good doctor or a good architect is a development of our mental capacity of reason. Even physical skills, such as carpentry, use the mind to realize how best to achieve their goals. Similarly, the challenge behind fishing is in part a mental exercise, and even the enjoyment of playing a game of baseball or football is not all physical; we direct our bodies with the understanding we have in our minds, for which reason we don't find animals playing games like baseball. In short, directing our actions through reason is itself a human fulfillment. We recognize a special accomplishment in using our understanding in order to achieve our goals, which is why we all naturally take pride and enjoyment in developing certain skills. To become good at something is profoundly satisfying. Unfortunately, many jobs in our society today are mindless and do little to fulfill human capacities. Someone on the factory line who drills the same screw thousands of times a day has thereby hardly developed his reasoning.

These various mental achievements, then, are fittingly called virtues. Literally a virtue refers to a strength, and both knowledge and skills are strengths. More precisely, we have seen that a virtue is a strong disposition to act well. A good doctor certainly is well disposed to heal, and a good architect is disposed to build; similarly, a mathematician is well disposed to understand mathematics. Each of these, then, is a virtue; it is a strength disposing us to our fulfillment as human beings.

Three Speculative Virtues

Thomas describes these virtues as intellectual virtues, as opposed to moral virtues. Intellectual virtues are perfections of the mind or reason, while moral virtues are perfections of our appetites or desires (I-II, 56, 3; I-II, 58, 3). Intellectual virtues help us to think well, moral virtues help us to desire well. Aquinas divides intellectual virtues into two general sorts, speculative and practical virtues (I-II, 57). Our reason, he says, has the capacity to understand the truth, but that truth may itself be used in the service of directing our activities. Speculative virtues strengthen our understanding of the truth as truth; practical virtues strengthen our application of the truth to activity. Knowledge of astronomy, for instance, is a speculative virtue, for it is concerned simply with understanding. Knowledge of architecture, on the other hand, is a practical virtue, for it is knowledge of how to do something.

Aquinas considers three kinds of speculative virtues: understanding, science, and wisdom (I-II, 57, 2). Understanding refers to a grasp of basic principles, the starting points of knowledge, while science refers to a grasp of the conclusions from these basic principles. As such, the word "science" does not correspond with our current usage, for today we have narrowed the use to refer to a particular mode of study involving experiments and mathematical measurements. Indeed, the current usage also seems to bring with it a whole tradition: someone is not a scientist unless he belongs to the community of scientists. As such, the study of theology or philosophy would not count as science. In contrast, for Aquinas theology is science par excellence (I, 1, 5). We need not get excited over the difference, for it is merely a difference in verbal usage. For Aquinas, "science" simply refers to a body of knowledge, whether or not it uses experiments or mathematical measurements.

We are not apt to distinguish sharply between understanding and science, but Thomas thought the distinction was fundamental, for the two involve different ways of knowing the truth. To us, what is all important is the distinction of subject matter, such as the difference between biology and physics. Thomas also recognized this distinction, but he thought the difference between understanding and science was more fundamental. Understanding is a grasp of the basic starting points; science is a grasp of the conclusions in light of these basic starting points. Understanding involves a simple grasp, an understanding of terms and what follows from them; science involves deductive reasoning. Science presupposes understanding, for we cannot reach conclusions without the principles, but understanding does not require science.

The third speculative virtue, wisdom, combines the other two in an overarching science of all reality, especially as it relates to God. Wisdom critically examines the basic starting points, and it examines all of the sciences, uniting everything under the single topic of being. Since God is the cause of all being, wisdom understands everything in its relation to God. Wisdom takes the grand perspective, considering not just this thing here or that thing there, but considering what is common to all things. Wisdom, you might say, puts all the pieces together. As long as we have only the individual sciences, we may fail to see the big picture; we may fail to see how it all fits together into a single whole.

Habits, Again

Like justice and like the virtues of the emotions, the speculative virtues are habits. They are strong dispositions to behave in a certain way. Yet they are not quite the same; they are dispositions giving us the capacity to act well, but they do not actually move us to act well (I-II, 56, 3). If I have a deep grasp of mathematics, having studied it for many years, then we may say that I have a disposition to understand mathematics. I find it very easy, even second nature, to think in mathematical terms; I can do it readily and with great success. But however good I am at mathematics, my habit does not move me to think mathematically. I must choose to think mathematically. In contrast, if I have a habit of justice, I will quite spontaneously desire to do the just thing. I still must choose, of course, and I might choose against my habit, but the habit itself gives rise to the desire. The intellectual habit of mathematics, on the other hand, does not spontaneously give rise to mathematical thoughts. I must first choose to think about mathematics, and then my habit is engaged.

This difference in habits follows from the subject of the habits. Mathematics is a habit of the mind, a power of understanding; justice is a habit of the appetites, a power of desire. While the mind gives us the ability to act, it does not move us to act; in contrast, the appetites are what propel us to act. It follows that a habit of the mind will give us a facility for acting well, while a habit of the appetites will not only give us the facility, it will itself propel us to act.

The intellectual habits might actually have the more fundamental meaning of "habit" (though the secondary meaning of "virtue"), for they are literally a kind of having. We say that I *have* knowledge of mathematics, an understanding to which I have ready access, something in storage that I can recall at will. In contrast, we are not apt to say that moderation is simply a *having* of right desire concerning bodily pleasures, a kind of storage of such desires. It is more than the having; it is the spontaneous use.

The greater our habit of a particular body of knowledge, the deeper and clearer is our understanding, and so the more firmly we hold to its truths. The mathematician not only finds thinking mathematically easier; he also has a deeper understanding of mathematical truths, and he is more sure of them than a beginner who grasps the very same truths (I, 85, 7). The more he thinks mathematically—using his mathematical knowledge—the deeper are the truths ingrained in his mind. What may be a faint etching in one person's mind becomes a bold outline to one who has the intellectual virtue.

Practical Virtues

Besides using our minds to understand the world around us, we also take this understanding and direct our own activities. An architect uses his knowledge to direct his activity of designing and building; a doctor uses his knowledge to direct his activity of healing. Aquinas calls this how-to knowledge "practical knowledge," and the corresponding virtues he calls practical virtues, of which there are two main types, art and prudence. By "art" he does not mean merely the drawing of paintings; he refers to any body of knowledge about how to make something (I-II, 57, 3). Medicine, architecture, and automotive mechanics are all arts. They are skills that involve an understanding of the subject matter to help bring about the desired result. Such knowledge, says Aquinas, is primarily directed not to the perfection of the mind but to the production of something to be made. In contrast, speculative knowledge is concerned primarily with perfecting the human mind.

Prudence we will also call practical wisdom, since the English word "prudence" has negative connotations associated with it. We will dwell at length upon prudence in the next chapter, so for the moment we will merely consider how it differs from art. Art directs our productive activity, which is ultimately completed in the product made, while practical wisdom directs the ordering of our own actions, our doings rather than our makings (I-II, 57, 4). Art is concerned with a good thing to be made; prudence is concerned with human actions done well. Art is concerned with the perfection of the product; practical wisdom is concerned with the perfection or fulfillment of the whole of human life (I-II, 21, 2, ad 2).

The study of ethics, then, is closely related to prudence, for both are concerned with our actions insofar as they are humanly fulfilling. Both are practical knowledge, for they tell us how to do something. Indeed, both will tell us which actions are good and which actions are evil. Nevertheless, the two are distinct from one another. They differ in two important characteristics.

First, ethics merely examines the general principles of good and evil actions, while practical wisdom applies this knowledge to the concrete situations of life (II-II, 47, 3). Ethics might tell us that we should repay our debts; prudence will tell us how we ought to go about repaying this particular debt that we have incurred. In a similar way, an architect must take his general knowledge of good construction (comparable to ethics) and apply it to the particular building that he is constructing (comparable to prudence).

Second, prudence is practical in the fullest sense, for it engages the person's appetites. A person might know a lot about ethics without caring a bit about doing what is good. Anna might have studied business ethics and know that embezzling is wrong, yet she does not care; if the opportunity arises, she might well desire what she knows to be wrong. A prudent person, on the other hand, not only knows the good, she desires it. She not only knows how to bring about the good, she actually seeks to bring it about. Consequently, practical wisdom is not only an intellectual virtue; it does double duty as a moral virtue as well (I-II, 58, 3, ad 1; II-II, 47, 1, ad 3). We will further examine this connection between prudence and desire in the next chapter.

Once again, both art and prudence are habits. They are the having of a certain knowledge. The architect has a ready understanding of building, as the doctor has a deep understanding of healing. Only by repeatedly thinking about the subject matter—and actually doing the activity—are the practical intellectual virtues developed.

Knowledge and the Moral Virtues

How do the intellectual virtues relate to the moral life? Common sense tells us that someone can have the intellectual virtues and be a reprehensible person. A brilliant scientist can be a liar and a swindler. A great doctor can be greedy and arrogant. There is no necessary connection between intellectual virtues and being good, with the exception of prudence (I-II, 58, 5). Indeed, the virtue of humility seems to have difficulty cohabitating with knowledge, which puffs up.

The opposite is also true: a very good person need not have the intellectual virtues (I-II, 58, 4). Although he must have the moral virtues, for he must be generous, patient, humble, and so on, he might not have the intellectual virtues (with the exception of practical wisdom, and says Aquinas, understanding, for he must understand the basic principles of the moral life). He might know little science, and he might not have any particular skills, yet he is a good person. In no way, then, do the intellectual virtues seem to be connected to the moral virtues. Someone can have the intellectual virtues without the moral virtues; someone else can have the moral virtues without the intellectual virtues.

This evident division between knowledge and being good, or between the intellectual virtues and the moral virtues, seems to pose a problem. For we have said that the ethical life is concerned with the good life, and the good life is what is fulfilling of human beings. We now discover that our fulfillment includes the intellectual virtues. It seems, then, that ethics, the knowledge of how to lead a fulfilling life, should tell us to pursue the intellectual virtues. How is it, then, that these virtues are so independent of being good?

We will approach this problem from two angles. First, we will show that the intellectual virtues are indeed part of the good life, but they can sometimes be possessed as if they were not; second, we will show that leading a good life does not require the accomplishment of the intellectual virtues, but it does require the love of these virtues.

Consider someone who is insensitive to his own good fortune. Suppose that he has a wonderful wife and a beautiful family, but he is unhappy because he is ambitious for political success. Nothing pleases him so long as he does not advance in the world. What are we to say of him? That he has no good thing in which he can rejoice? Of course not. He has much with which to be pleased. Rather, we say that he does not know how to rejoice in the good that he has. He has something good—a beautiful family—but he does not really possess it as a good, for he does not appreciate its true worth. In order to possess a good truly as a good we must not only have it; in addition, we must love it as good (I-II, 34, 4 ad 3; I-II, 56, 3).

Such is the condition of the intellectual goods. They are certainly human goods, even as a family is a true good. But someone might have them without appreciating them for their true worth. Someone might fail to love them as she ought. For instance, a doctor might love the skill of medicine only insofar as it gets her money. We should not deny that the money is good, and we get money from jobs; but a doctor who loves her skill only for the money fails to love it as the fulfillment of her human capacity to reason. She does not fully possess it, then, as the human good that it is. Similarly, someone might be a brilliant scientist, but he cherishes his knowledge only because he hopes that others will praise him for his learning. He has the intellectual virtue of science, but he doesn't possess it as a good fulfilling of his human capacities. He is like the man who doesn't appreciate his family for its true worth.

Ultimately, if we are to possess the intellectual virtues as a true human good, then we must love them as fitting within the overall human good, including the common good, which we considered in connection with justice. Knowledge, for instance, must be loved as ordered to the good of the whole, and art must be loved not simply as my good but as part of the good of the whole (II-II, 186, 1; 180, 2, ad 1).

We can have the intellectual virtues without being good because the intellectual virtues do not carry with them the appropriate love. Someone can have knowledge without loving it as he ought, just as someone can have a wife without loving her for her true worth. It follows that the intellectual virtues are true goods, even as a wonderful family is truly a blessing, but they are not always possessed as good. They can be loved for something besides their true good, even as knowledge might be loved for vainglory. The intellectual virtues, then, have only half of what it takes for something to be truly fulfilling. They have the good, but they do not necessarily have the love.

It is little wonder, then, that the intellectual virtues are detached from being good. To be truly good, a person not only must have a good, he must love it as he ought. The brilliant scientist not only must have knowledge, he must love the knowledge as fitting into the whole of human perfection. If he selfishly clings to his knowledge as a private good solely for his own gain, then he has something good, but he himself is not good, for he does not love the good as he ought.

In contrast, the moral virtues have the appropriate love built into them. Someone is just only if he loves his neighbor and only if he seeks justice as a true human good. Suppose someone refrains from stealing only because he is afraid of being caught. Such a man has done the just thing—for he did not steal—but he does not have the virtue of justice, for he does not love justice as good in itself. We can say, then, that someone has the intellectual virtue of science but does not love it as he ought, but we cannot say that someone has the moral virtue of justice but fails to love it as he ought. The intellectual virtue remains without the love; justice does not. Similarly, the other moral virtues have right desire built into them. Someone is not generous unless he loves to give out of a true love for others. If he gives only for a tax deduction or because he hopes for favors in return, then he lacks the virtue of generosity.

We have addressed the first concern: someone can have the intellectual virtues without being good, for while the intellectual virtues are certainly a human perfection, they need not be loved as part of the true human good. What of the second concern, that someone can be morally good without possessing the intellectual virtues? How is it, if the intellectual virtues are part of the good life, that someone can be good without being knowledgeable or without having reasoned skills?

The intellectual virtues are not so wholly separate from being good as we initially suppose. While someone can be good without having the intellectual virtues, a connection remains between being good and the intellectual virtues, for a good person will still love the intellectual virtues, even if he has not attained them, and even if he doesn't have the mental capacity to attain them. A good person, for instance, holds the truth in regard. He does not despise the truth, but recognizes it as a true human good. Among the moral virtues, Aquinas includes the virtue of studiousness, which is the appropriate pursuit of the truth (II-II, 161). Someone cannot be truly good if he disdains the truth. Aquinas also discusses a vice or sin called sloth or laziness, which is the failure to pursue spiritual goods because of the unwillingness to sacrifice bodily goods (II-II, 35). This vice, thinks Aquinas, is the primary obstacle to pursuing the truth. It is also an obstacle to developing one's talents and skills, for a good person will not neglect his talents but will develop them as he is able. While a good person may have few skills, he certainly will not be lazy. He will love the intellectual virtue of art as a spiritual good worth pursuing.

Still, actually acquiring the intellectual virtues is not necessary for someone to be good (except, says Aquinas, prudence and understanding of ethical principles). True, he must love the intellectual virtues; he must pursue them insofar as he is able and insofar as his lot in life demands it, but their possession is not necessary for someone to be good. He might love the truth but simply lack the mental capacity to understand very much. We are good, says Aquinas, through the use we make of things, not through the gifts we are given (I, 48, 6). Someone who is given one thousand dollars but uses it well is better than someone who is given five thousand dollars but uses it poorly. If someone lacks the intellectual capacity to understand, then he is good, and shares in the good life, insofar as he loves the truth and loves the understanding that others attain.

The Human Good of Truth

Ethics does not primarily consist in a list of dos and don'ts, but rather in the directives of how to live a humanly good life. As such, ethics includes not only the moral virtues, which put our appetites in order, but also the intellectual virtues, which are the perfections of what Aristotle calls that divine element within us, the ability to reason and so to understand the truth. In our own day, when Pilate's question, "What is truth?" is on everyone's lips, we are greatly hindered from achieving this truly divine and human perfection. Widespread skepticism undermines our appreciation of the truth, and a prevalent materialism saps our love of spiritual goods. Happiness will not be found where our society looks, in material and bodily goods; it will be found only in spiritual goods, including the good of knowledge.

12

Practical Wisdom

❧

Knowledge without justice ought to be called
cunning rather than wisdom.

Plato

Making Practical Judgments

We have already suggested that ethics is more than resolving complicated moral questions, for even after the questions are answered, the choices must be made. Those choices, we have seen, will be heavily influenced by our habits of desiring. As I stand in the bank holding the teller's extra twenty dollars, I may judge that I should return the extra money, but if I am greedy, then I am likely to take it anyway. Still, you might insist, *part* of ethics is figuring out what is to be done. And so it is. A class discussing a thorny moral issue, then, is not wasted. It might help develop those mental skills necessary to make good moral judgments.

But we must avoid a simplistic division between judging what is to be done and doing it, as if the first were wholly a mental activity and the second were wholly a volitional or affective activity. The two are in fact intertwined, so that one cannot be wholly disentangled from the other. Judgment is not entirely mental but involves an affective element, and choice is ineffectual without the guidance of reason.

The virtue of practical wisdom, sometimes called prudence, bridges the boundary between mental judgment and affective desire. Moderation and courage are in the emotions; justice is in the will; practical wisdom, on the other hand, is a virtue of reason (II-II, 47, 1). It is right reason about things to be done. But while it resides most properly in reason, which judges what is to be done and commands its execution, practical wisdom rests upon the affective virtues, for clear-sighted judgment can be made only with right desire, and the execution of the deed can be carried out only with a firm will.

Discussing moral issues and particular cases, then, will not necessarily develop good judgment. No doubt such discussions provide assistance, chiefly in considering the many circumstances and ramifications of our actions. But ultimately they cannot provide good reasoning, which presupposes right desire or appetite. Indeed, their abstraction from sound principles and right desire may engender a disregard for the true goods that are found in reality, substituting a kind of relativism of judgment that we have already examined. We will see that truly good judgment, realized in the virtue of practical wisdom, is rooted in principle and applied through experience, with a love of the true good.

Three Acts of Prudence

According to Thomas the virtue of prudence has three primary acts: counsel, judgment, and command (II-II, 47, 8). In the act of counsel we consider our current situation and assess the options before us. In the act of judgment we determine which of the options is best. Finally, we must command ourselves to do it. Many have successfully completed the first two tasks, ably considering the merit of each of their options and then judging which is to be done, but have lingered, unable to bring themselves fully to do it. They judge what is to be done, almost in an abstract way, but do not direct themselves to it. They have failed in the consummation of practical wisdom, so that however well they take counsel and judge, they will be far from wise.

The first two actions are what Thomas calls speculative, for their primary concern is to judge the truth of the matter, but the third action is properly practical, for it applies reason to the action itself. The first two, therefore, are wholly acts of reason, although they enlist the aid of desire, while command is an act of reason mixed with will; it is the direction of reason together with the impetus of will (II-II, 47, 8). We should note that the word "speculative" is used in a slightly different manner than it was in the last chapter, in which it concerned knowing the truth just for the sake of understanding. Both counsel and judgments are not speculative in this sense. They are ultimately concerned with knowing how to act. Nevertheless, they lack the most complete sense of practical knowledge, because they are not bound up with the will to act, as is command. We can judge the truth of how to act without having the desire that moves us to act.

Suppose, for instance, that Clare, who manages a factory, must decide whether to blow the whistle on the owner of the factory, Louis, who has sidestepped some federal regulations regarding worker safety. She begins by taking counsel. What are her options and what are the merits of each? She might simply keep her mouth shut and go on with her life; she might bring the matter to Louis's attention, hoping to persuade him to change his ways; or she might report Louis to the appropriate authorities. If she takes the first option, then she will be partially responsible for any injuries that befall her workers; therefore, she must determine how great a risk the workers face. She is not too hopeful of the success of the second option, and besides, she fears that Louis might be upset and dismiss her. The third option may indeed bring the factory up to appropriate safety standards, but she has little doubt that Louis would suspect her, and her job would be in great jeopardy. She does not think it would be easy to get another job, and she has three children to care for.

Notice that her counsel involves many factors. She must assess the current situation: exactly what laws have been broken; how much risk do the workers face; how much does she currently need this job. She must also project into the future: will Louis listen to her; will she lose her job; will the safety measures be implemented? She must also judge the value of certain things: is it more important that she keep this job or that the workers have a safe environment?

The second step is judgment, in which she must determine which option is best. This final judgment often depends upon details that may be simply unavailable in a brief case study as we have presented here, but let us suppose that she should blow the whistle on Louis. Next, she must give command. Not only must she say, "Reporting Louis to Occupational Safety and Health Administration is the best thing"; she must also direct herself, "Report Louis." And here she may falter. Hamlet had judged that he should kill his stepfather and so end the reign of a tyrant, but then he wavered; he did not command himself to act, and he reconsidered his judgment; and he reconsidered again, and again, until it was nearly too late. Similarly, Clare might waver. She might resolve to report Louis, but then procrastinate. She might reconsider her situation and decide that, after all, perhaps she should just remain quiet. By failing in the act of command, she would then lack the essence of practical wisdom.

Experience

Both counsel and judgment require more than book knowledge. True enough, Clare must be aware of some basic principles, such as the following: she must provide for her children, she must protect the rights of those under her charge, and wrong-doing must be punished. But these abstract principles will hardly suffice to tell Clare what she should do. She must be able to apply these principles to her own life, to the concrete decision that she faces, and such application requires experience in making good choices (II-II, 49, 1, especially ad 1; II-II, 47, 3).

We see the same sort of thing in other areas, such as medicine, where judgments are complex and uncertain. In order for a doctor to have good judgment, he certainly needs book knowledge of diseases, their symptoms, and their cures. But he needs more than the book knowledge. He needs hands-on experience of applying his knowledge to individual patients. Diagnosing an illness through its symptoms can be a tricky matter; a mere memorization of the disease and its symptoms will hardly suffice. Determining the best treatment for an illness already diagnosed can also be difficult. Again, book knowledge does not suffice; experience is needed as well. We build this experience into the very training of our doctors, who must serve as interns and residents in order to apply their knowledge to individual patients. We are also apt to include this experience in our assessment of a doctor. We may be more inclined to go to an experienced doctor rather than to one fresh out of school.

The same sort of experience is needed for practical wisdom. Knowing what is right and wrong, having a list of dos and don'ts, is hardly adequate for good counsel and correct judgment. We have to apply this knowledge to the decisions we face, which requires experience. We need experience to recall what has resulted from similar situations in the past, which Aquinas calls memory (II-II, 49, 1). We need experience to realize when a certain action falls under an injunction or norm, which Aquinas calls understanding, not to be confused with the understanding discussed last chapter (II-II, 49, 2, especially ad 1). Furthermore, we need experience to foresee the ramifications of our actions, which Aquinas calls providence or foresight (II-II, 49, 6).

A PhD in ethics, then, does not make for practical wisdom. It might help, but it is no guarantor. Knowledge is the first step in practical wisdom, but its application takes experience. We should not look to the young, then, for prudence, except in cases of divine inspiration, for the young have little experience in life and little experience making good choices. We imagine a wise person as wrinkled and graying. Much can be said for this stereotype, for only the aged have had the greatest opportunity to acquire practical wisdom.

Principles

Case studies are most helpful in the area of counsel, for they often allow us to see many sides of a situation, and they may even provide a kind of vicarious experience to help us evaluate the options. They cannot, however, provide what is presupposed to any good counsel or judgment, namely, foundational moral principles. Although knowledge of these principles is separate from prudence, no one can be wise without this knowledge, which Aquinas calls *synderesis,* for which there is no good translation, except the cumbersome phrase "knowledge of the principles of ethics" (II-II, 47, 6). Since *synderesis* is understanding of principles, it belongs to the speculative virtue of understanding discussed last chapter. We will be more concerned with a detailed examination of *synderesis* later, but for the moment we wish to see at least that counsel without principles is not prudence; at best it is mere cleverness.

Students in ethics classes have been asked to discuss an astounding array of cases, not all of which are worthy of consideration. Should a student cheat on a test? Should someone have relations before he is married? Should a woman have an abortion? These are questions that could be settled with a quick application of some basic principles: do not cheat; do not fornicate; and do not kill innocent human life (I-II, 14, 4). If the principles are known, there is nothing to be discussed. But if the principles are not known, then the cases seem open game for evaluation.

We might suppose that we know better now: we can't judge what is best for others; furthermore, not everything is black and white. Why else do we take counsel?

But some things are black and white, a truth that we still acknowledge in our own day. Indeed, we are not all that different from Aquinas. Imagine a discussion, in our day, about whether someone should continue hiring based upon race, or imagine a discussion on a case in which a man must decide whether or not to beat his wife. Fundamental principles, we would suppose, preclude deliberation over such matters. To even consider the options indicates a deplorable lack of sensitivity. Or, perhaps, a deplorable lack of prudence. Similarly, to even consider adultery, fornication, or murder of the unborn is the antithesis of practical wisdom.

Even in less certain cases, where the decision does require counsel, the principles are presupposed. How can Clare deliberate over safeguarding her workers if she does not realize that we all have a fundamental obligation to care for others? If she fails to understand, like many in our modern world, that a regard for other people is a true good, then how can she even consider the issue at hand? We can't throw her into the lion's den of counsel and deliberation without giving her the weapons of moral principles. Otherwise, she is sure to fail. Counsel without principles—however perspicacious, however exhaustive, however subtle—is not good counsel. Even less can judgment be good without principles.

No relativistic discussion of cases, therefore, can ever develop practical wisdom, which must be rooted in *synderesis*. The question is not so much, "What do you think should be done?" as "What do the principles lead us to conclude?" Prudence is not a lot of talk and consideration apart from the clear principles of morals; it is the application of those principles to the concrete decisions we face in our lives.

Right Desire

Perhaps the most important prerequisite to prudence is neither experience nor principles but right desire. To the modern mind, it is also the most surprising. We have already indicated the inadequacy of viewing morals as a matter of being clever in resolving complex issues, for after the judgment is made, the choice must yet follow. Unfortunately, that choice may not follow so much upon what we know is right as upon what we desire. Right desire, then, is important in the moral life, because it undergirds right choice. But it also underlies right judgment itself.

"The heart has its reasons, which reason does not know," says Pascal. While he was speaking of religious faith, what he says might also be applied to practical wisdom, for when it comes to perceiving good and evil, two sorts of judgments are possible: a dry intellectual judgment that something is good or evil, or a judgment of the heart (I, 1, 6, ad 3). One person might judge that pornography is an evil to be avoided. Another person might be repulsed by the very idea of pornography. Both have perceived that pornography is evil, one with his head and the other with his heart. Or consider two ways that we might know a person. We might know many facts about him, as a historian might know about George Washington, or we might know him personally; we might know him not only with our heads but also with our hearts.

When Clare is assessing the merits of her many options, she uses various intellectual judgments about the importance of goods to be pursued. She might also, however, rely upon the judgments of her heart. Perhaps her indignation at cheating, her compassion for the misfortune of others, and her disdain for mere human approval, will decide the issue for her. By desiring what is good, she comes to know what is good; by hating evil, she comes to realize its depravity. As we have noted, desire follows knowledge; now we see that knowledge follows desire.

The role of the affections within moral knowledge is not perfectly clear, but Aquinas indicates that we might well trust more the judgment of someone whose heart is in the right place, rather than someone who is very knowledgeable (I, 1, 6). I suspect that the heart does not so much provide the awareness *that* something is good, for desire presupposes knowledge of the good, but rather it provides awareness of *how* good it is. Strength of desire affects the importance we give to certain considerations.

When discussing prudence, Thomas focuses more upon another role of right desire, namely, that we keep focused upon the proper goal. Practical wisdom, he says, does not concern itself with the end or goal, but with the means of achieving that goal (II-II, 47, 6). Prudence presupposes the end, so that anyone who loses focus on the goal, however clever he is at discovering means, will not be wise. When I am deciding whether to return that extra twenty dollars, I must keep in mind my goal in relation to the bank, which is justice, and the proper goal of desiring money, which is to desire what reason judges best. If I long to take the money I may forget these goals. I might set as a goal the inordinate acquisition of money; I might set as a goal not justice but whatever serves my self-interest.

Our desires set the goals that we deliberate over, so that if our desires are out of order, seeking an inappropriate end, then our deliberation will itself be skewed. Consider the situation where I am at the bank and the teller has given me an extra twenty-dollar bill, and then recall our earlier discussion of rationalization. We begin by knowing what we should do, as I might begin knowing that I should return the money. But we then desire what in fact is wrong, as I desire to take the money. Finally, we try to justify our evil desire in quasi-moral terms. Notice what has happened. My evil desires set me off on another goal, not the moral goal. No matter how much I deliberate on this disordered goal of unrestrained acquisition of money, I cannot reach the proper moral judgment. Neither, then, can I be wise. Memory, understanding, and foresight in the service of a bad end are not prudence but mere cleverness.

Bad desires, then, lead us astray from the rightful end, dragging us into pursuit of what is inappropriate. Since prudence presupposes the end, and passes judgment only upon the means, there can be no practical wisdom where the end is lacking. But as long as our desires seek what is unreasonable, we will sometimes be led astray. Complete prudence, then, presupposes the proper ordering of our desires. If we desire what is right, then we will deliberate over the right ends. But if our desires are errant, then we will sometimes turn our reason toward calculating the best way to satisfy our unreasonable impulses.

A Circle of Growth

The striking conclusion is that practical wisdom presupposes the other virtues. Just so long as we lack moderation, for instance, we will sometimes desire improper bodily pleasures; consequently, we may set our reason at the service of our emotions, as values clarification would have us do. Only if we are fully moderate, so that our appetites readily follow the judgment of reason, will we be free from rationalization, pursuing always the proper goal. Again, just so long as we lack courage, we will sometimes fear what we should not, and so rationalize our own cowardice, thereby subverting the proper end and setting up a goal of simply satisfying our emotions, which have been spurred on by the presentation of the imagination. The same may be said of patience, generosity, humility, and the other virtues. If they are not in place, then neither is prudence in place (I-II, 65, 1).

Paradoxically, the opposite is true as well: we cannot have the moral virtues if we do not have prudence. Recall that moderation is the habit of desiring according to the judgment of reason. Moderation, then, presupposes a proper judgment of reason. If that judgment is lacking, then so is moderation. We have seen, however, that the proper judgment of reason concerning what is to be done arises from the virtue of prudence. Without practical wisdom, then, there is no moderation. Similarly, courage is the habit of fearing and braving according to the judgment of reason, a judgment that comes through prudence. Wherever there is a moral virtue, so too there must be prudence.

We might wonder, then, how we can ever attain the virtues. We cannot become moderate unless we are wise, but we cannot become wise unless we are moderate. How, then, can we get started? Thomas is not troubled by this seeming paradox. It merely means, says he, that the virtues must grow together (I-II, 66, 2). If we have a modicum of practical wisdom, then we can have a modicum of moderation. By increasing our moderation, we also increase our practical wisdom, which will in turn help to increase moderation and the other virtues. We must keep in mind that we attain the virtues by degrees. We are not either wise or unwise; rather, we are wise to some degree. We are not either moderate or immoderate; rather, we are moderate to some degree. To the degree that we have moderation, we have a measure of practical wisdom, and by increasing our moderation, we also increase our practical wisdom.

Command

The last act of prudence, command, also presupposes right desire, especially in the will. Indeed, incorporated within the very act of command is a firm act of will (I-II, 17, 1). What is most opposed to the act of command is an indecisiveness, arising from a divided heart. Singleness of mind—by which we mean singleness of heart—is the essential feature of command. If I am divided in my longings, then I am not likely to command myself, or at least I will give only a half-hearted command; after all, only half my heart is in it. If I have judged that I should return the extra twenty dollars, but I retain a secret longing to keep the money for myself, then I may not direct myself to act. Or I may do so with little force, so that when my greed arises again I will hesitate and pull my hand back, reconsidering my options. Rather than saying to myself, "Return the money," I might instead say, "I really ought to return the money." The force of the first statement has been drained from the second, leaving only a feeble directive.

We all know that we are not likely to follow the directives of a boss or leader who is indecisive. Someone who gives only suggestions and never orders is likely to be ignored in the long run. Similarly, if we give ourselves only suggestions, we are not likely to listen to ourselves. When we make a decision we must stand wholly behind it. We must march forward to do the right thing and not look back at our inordinate desires. Noble goals are not attained by forever regretting that we must sacrifice lesser things. Only by unity of purpose will we achieve the sublime end of the moral life.

13

Ethics and Knowledge

*True law is right reason in agreement with nature; it is
of universal application, unchanging and everlasting;
it summons to duty by its commands, and averts from
wrongdoing by its prohibitions.*

Cicero

How Do We Know What Is Right and Wrong?

In our discussion of ethics we have asserted that some things are
right and others wrong. We have said, for instance, that we ought
to have fair exchanges with others, that we ought to conform our
desires with reason, and that we ought to work toward the common good. We have said that we should not kill the innocent,
that we should not steal, and that we should not lie. How is it, you
might wonder, that we can know all these things? Indeed, how
can anyone know what is right and wrong? After all, disagree-
ments over moral questions abound. Different societies have different beliefs, and even our own society has a plethora of views.
Some say that we should not kill the innocent, while others say

that we can, in the form of euthanasia or abortion. Some say that sexual relations should be reserved for marriage, and others say that anything goes, just so long as there is consent. Some say that capital punishment is wrong; others that it has a part to play in society. Amidst this cacophony, one struggles even to hear oneself think. Perhaps it is best, amidst such confusion, to throw up our hands and acknowledge that we simply cannot know what is right and wrong. People have forever disagreed and will forever disagree. Let each one hold his own opinion.

Such a view is not a wholesale relativism of values; it does not deny the possibility of some true right and wrong. But it is a relativism of our knowledge; whatever the truth, we will never know it. Some people make the same claim about God. There is some truth about God—either he exists or he does not—but we will never know what the truth is. The reason given here is much the same as with morals: people disagree about God, so we simply cannot say what is correct.

Rationalizations, Again

Is disagreement really a good measure of whether we can know something? People disagree over just about everything. Members of the Flat Earth Society, for instance, think that the earth is flat and that a worldwide conspiracy attempts to fool us all into thinking the earth is round. Because of this disagreement should we conclude that we can't know the truth of the matter? Or rather, should we conclude that people are very good at disagreeing, even when the answer is available?

People are especially good at disagreeing over morals, but not because we can't know the truth of the matter. Rather, the root of much moral disagreement seems to lie in our propensity to rationalize (I-II, 94, 6). We have already seen that a rationalization involves three steps: (1) we know what is right or wrong; (2) we want what is wrong; and (3) we come up with a quasi-moral reason for doing what is wrong. Step one begins with knowing morals, and if we stopped there we might well have moral agreement. But by the time we reach step three we have abandoned our knowledge in preference for confusion, a confusion that might well lead to disagreement. When a whole society begins to rationalize along the same lines, then we end up with disagreement between societies.

Consider, for instance, some of the rationale for slavery in the antebellum South. Among other things, it was suggested that those of African blood were defective human beings, so that they could not take care of themselves, or that abolishing slavery would ruin the economy and so do more harm to African Americans than good. Perhaps these arguments were advanced in complete sincerity. But on the other hand, perhaps they were the quasi-moral reasons produced by rationalizations. The slave owners, realizing that slavery was wrong but wanting to own slaves nevertheless, came up with rationalizations for their deeds. The result was disagreement. Why? Because they could not know what was right or wrong? No. In fact, they began by knowing what was right, but disagreement arose from a failure in desires. The slave owners desired what was wrong, and so ended up confusing themselves. Much moral disagreement might arise in this manner. Our weakness lies not so much in our moral knowledge as in our desires.

Besides the moral confusion arising from our evil desires, Thomas points to another confusion that arises from custom or argument (I-II, 94, 6). In other words, although we can know what is right, we are misled by our societal upbringing. He does not mean that we are bound by our training, as if we could not rise above our upbringing—history points to many people who have—but that societal standards will make the truth more difficult to discover, so that many people will simply comply with their culture. The two sorts of confusion, of course, might well be related. What began as a rationalization following upon evil desires might later be taught in a society, so that later generations are confused by custom.

How, Not Whether

When it comes to moral truths the question should not be *whether* we know right and wrong, but *how* we know right and wrong. That we know some moral truths is granted by everyone, if not in their words, then at least in their thoughts. That we should not rape, that we should not discriminate based upon race, that we should not frame the innocent, that we should not steal to make our fortune, that we should not follow blind desires are truths that anyone will grant. The following moral truths are known as well (with the caveat that circumstances might make these actions evil, e.g., if they were done for an evil motive): we should help those in need; we should tell the truth; we should take care of our children; we should love others.

That we know moral truths is not in doubt; *how* we know them is the real question. While we certainly know that we should feed the hungry, we don't come to our knowledge just by looking with our eyes. Nor does a scientific analysis of hunger and nutrition supply the knowledge. We know that discrimination is wrong not merely by descriptions of people's skin color, or even by descriptions of their culture. How, then, do we know that these things are wrong?

Nature versus Nurture

Is it just a matter of what we have been taught? Some people claim that our moral beliefs just depend upon what our parents and our society have taught us. They seem to conclude that our moral beliefs are merely a matter of blind faith.

Surely what they say has some truth, for we have been taught moral truths, and without this teaching our knowledge might be deficient. Our parents taught us to share with others, not to harm others, and so on. But the same point might be made of mathematics. How do we come to know that $5^2 = 25$? No doubt, we begin by believing our teachers. Fortunately, it does not stop there. At some point, the light goes on and we see it for ourselves. We have moved from mere belief to understanding. We may have never reached this point of understanding, however, had we been taught mathematical error. We do now understand, but our understanding was aided by proper teaching.

The same process takes place in morals. We begin by believing authorities, such as our parents. But just as our minds come to understand mathematical truths, so our minds come to understand moral truths. Our parents tell us that we must share, and we concede the point, perhaps reluctantly. At a later time, however, we come to see the truth of what our parents have told us. Similarly, we know that rape is wrong in part because of what we have been taught—and with a deficient upbringing our beliefs might be confused—but nevertheless, we *do* know that rape is wrong, and our knowledge rests upon the nature of the action, not merely upon blind trust in those that instructed us; at some point we come to perceive the truth of the matter.

Another prevalent view is that we are just born with moral knowledge; we all naturally have an internal voice telling what is right and wrong, an inborn conscience to guide us. If *inborn* means we are actually born with the knowledge, the way we are born with two arms, two legs, and a head, then Aquinas disagrees with this view (I-II, 51, 1). The knowledge is not present when we are born; we must discover it. Still, Aquinas would agree that our fundamental moral knowledge is natural, for we quite naturally discover it, the way that we discover mathematics or that objects no longer in view nevertheless continue to exist (I-II, 63, 1; I-II, 51, 1). There are some fundamental moral truths, says Aquinas, that we cannot help discovering. That we should be fair to others, that we should follow the guidance of reason rather than the blind impulse of passion, and that we should not harm others are all basic truths discovered naturally.

Aquinas, then, has both nature and nurture. We have a mind by which we can naturally discover the truth, including the truth about morals. Unfortunately, our minds are weak, so that we usually need assistance in coming to the truth. Typically, therefore, we begin by believing others, who teach us the truth. As we reflect upon the matter, however, we often move from belief to understanding. The natural capacity of our minds grasps what was previously only believed.

Discovering the Truth

These truths are not proven, any more than we prove that two and one make three. Rather, when we understand the subject matter, then we comprehend these truths. When we understand what a whole is and what a part is, we realize that a part is not greater than the whole (I-II, 94, 2). Or when we understand the role of an eye (to see) and what it means to be blind, then we understand that a blind eye fails in the purpose of an eye. Similarly, when we understand what it means to harm others, then we realize that we should not do it. In short, these truths belong to that speculative virtue of understanding discussed previously. In particular, they belong to what we have called *synderesis*.

We have seen something of how this understanding works. We realize, for instance, that we are human beings with the capacity to reason, and then we grasp that understanding the truth fulfills our capacities. We realize that our emotions need not blindly follow the impressions of imagination, and then we perceive that we act most fully as humans when we guide our emotions by the light of reason. We realize that other people share the human good with us, and then we understand that they are our equals, those who participate in our good rather than those that serve our good. Whenever we come to grasp some human propensity, we then perceive that its fulfillment is a human good.

Aquinas puts it in the following manner: when we understand some natural inclination, then we naturally grasp its object as good (I-II, 94, 2). What does Aquinas mean by "natural inclination"? In our day, by "natural inclination" we are apt to mean inborn emotional desires; for instance, if a certain sexual desire is thought to be inborn, then we call it natural. When Aquinas speaks of natural inclinations, however, he cannot possibly mean mere emotional desires. If so, his view would be indistinguishable from values clarification, which says that what we happen to desire is a value to us. Indeed, values clarification may even go so far as to say that our *natural* desires, as opposed to those thrust upon us by society, provide our true values.

Thomas would disagree. Some of our *natural* emotional desires—if by "natural" is meant "inborn"—are not good but evil. The role of the emotions is not to determine the good, but to conform to the good discovered by reason. Indeed, Aquinas says that the truly natural inclination of the emotions is to follow reason (I-II, 94, 2, ad 2). Before the emotions can desire what is reasonably good, therefore, reason must have first discovered the good. Since reason discovers the good from a grasp of our natural inclinations, the natural inclinations must themselves precede our emotional desires.

Perhaps Aquinas means by "inclination" nothing other than the natural capacities that we have been discussing, such as the ability to reason, to love with the will, and so on. The word "inclination" has something more of an active sense than "capacity." If we have a capacity, it means that we are able to do something, but if we have an inclination, it means that we are moving out to do it or at least that we are disposed to do it. Aquinas uses this more active sense, for he understands that we are, through our capacities, *directed* to achieve their fulfillment (I-II, 91, 2). None of us would suppose that our emotions are mere *abilities* to feel or desire. The very capacity of our emotions itself propels us on to act. Aquinas thought the same of our other capacities. Our reason is not merely an ability to grasp the truth; it is an endeavor toward the truth. After all, it is engaged quite spontaneously, even apart from our choices.

How do we become aware of these inclinations? Not by a subjective introspective experience, as values clarification says that we should become aware of our true feelings. We become aware of our natural inclinations not by searching our inner longings; rather, we become aware of them the same way that we become aware of the inclination of a rock, which is to fall, or the inclination of a cat, which is to hunt, namely, by observing behavior. When we see that we are the sorts of things that reason, then we understand that we are inclined to reason (I, 16, 4, ad 2; I, 77, 3). When we see that we are the sorts of animals that socialize, then we understand that we have an inclination to interact with others. And so on. Matters are not so simple, no doubt, for human behavior is very complex. But the fundamental idea is the following: by observing behavior, we realize inclination; upon knowing inclination, we naturally discover the good.

These inclinations, however, are not the whole story. Thomas says that the will is itself naturally inclined to the good of each of these human capacities; for instance, we have a natural love for the truth as grasped by reason (I-II, 10, 1). Why? Because the will is inclined to any and all human goods, and the fulfillment of our capacities—our inclinations—is a human good. Recall that the will is a rational appetite, that is, a loving and desiring power that follows upon reason's perception of the good. As such, the will desires goodness itself; it desires all things under the formality of good. When reason comes to understand that understanding the truth completes a natural capacity, then the will naturally desires this good.

We have, then, two layers. First, we perceive the natural capacity or propensity to some fulfillment, such as the mind's propensity to the truth, from which we grasp a human good, for example, understanding the truth is good. Then we desire this good with our will. Upon perceiving this desire of the will, we then grasp that understanding the truth is good. Are we simply repeating our grasp of this same good? No. The second time we are grasping it as a true human good, that is, as the object of a human act. Understanding the truth nonvoluntarily—without engaging the will—would be only an act of a human being, as discussed in chapter 10. What we perceive—following the natural inclination of the will—is that understanding the truth, as a human act, is a human good.

Aquinas speaks of procreation and education of offspring

as part of a natural inclination and therefore as human goods. Does he mean procreation as a natural capacity—shared with animals and plants—to propagate the species? Or does he mean an inclination of the will to human acts of procreation? The latter, it would seem. But this latter inclination only follows upon a perception of the former, that is, upon the perception of the natural capacity of reproduction. From this single natural capacity, we perceive diverse human goods reached through human actions. The completion of the natural capacity is a mature human being. This complete good is reached first through the act of procreation, which brings the individual into existence, and later through human acts of raising the child, which lead the child to maturity. The single natural capacity gives rise to multiple natural inclinations of the will.

The Moral Law and Obligation

But how do we get to right and wrong? How do we get to moral obligation? After all, it is one thing to say that understanding the truth is a human good; it is another to say that we ought to pursue the truth. It is one thing to say that others are our equals; it is another to say that we ought to treat them fairly. Up to this point we have explained how we come to grasp the human good, but we have not explained why we ought to pursue the good. How do we get from the knowledge of what is good to the idea that we ought to pursue the good?

The move is not difficult. Anybody can see that if you want some good, then you should pursue it. If you want to lose weight, then go on a diet; if you want to win at a race, then train hard. Any time we want some good, we readily perceive that we should work to attain it. So once we have grasped the human good, we see that we ought to pursue it.

Perhaps this reasoning is too weak. After all, it seems to leave room for someone to opt out of morality. Just as someone can opt out of the command "Go on a diet" simply by abandoning the desire to lose weight, or someone can ignore "Train hard" if they do not wish to win the race, so it seems that someone can opt out of the precept "Pursue the human good" simply by abandoning the human good. Someone might well say, "I acknowledge that truth is a good, but I don't care. I prefer to pursue other goods in its place, such as pleasure." Such a person, it seems, will have reached the first step—judging that truth is good—but will not move to the second step of judging that he ought to pursue the truth.

If we think that we ought to be able to hold him to morality more firmly, that we ought to be able to *oblige* him to follow the true human good, then we are in the company of Immanuel Kant, that great deontologist discussed previously. He understood that when you want some goal or end, then you direct yourself to pursue the means. If you want to lose weight, then you might give yourself the command "Go on a diet." He recognized that this command has force and influences your behavior only insofar as you want the goal of losing weight; if you give up the goal of losing weight, then the directive "Go on a diet" loses its efficacy. Kant called these commands hypothetical imperatives, for they depend upon the supposition of the end.

The trouble, which Kant sensed so keenly, is that hypothetical imperatives hold sway only so long as the person maintains the goal. Should he give up the goal, then he is released from the obligation. It seemed to Kant that morality should have more force to it; people should not be able to opt out of morality by opting out of the moral end, the way you might opt out of a diet by abandoning your desire to lose weight. People should be bound by the moral law no matter what goals they have; even the greatest evildoer is still bound by morality, although he has long since abandoned any moral goal.

In order to give morality this universal force, Kant turned to another imperative, the categorical imperative, which he deemed absolutely binding, not dependent upon any goal for its force. "Do not steal," for instance, is binding for all human beings no matter the goals they happen to have. Or "Develop your talents" has force independently of someone's desires. In Kant's mind, the categorical imperative corresponds with the moral law, to which all are obliged. The mere force of the law, apart from particular ends or goals, generates its own obligation.

Thomas has little room for a categorical imperative. In his mind, all obligations are hypothetical, depending upon some end or goal (I-II, 99, 1). He has no imperative "Seek the truth" hanging in midair with nothing to ground it. Rather, he has the good of truth, from which we perceive that we should pursue the truth. The command or precept depends upon the good after the manner of a hypothetical imperative.

Does it follow that all of morality is tentative, hanging upon the condition of right desire? Is all of morality a kind of hypothetical reasoning, such as, "If you want the good then pursue it," or "If you want the truth, then seek it"? Is everyone left with the option of abandoning morality, so that he might say, "I don't want the good, so I need not pursue it," or "Who cares about the truth, so I won't seek it"? Is morality just for those who happen to desire the true good, or is it binding for everyone, even those who have preferred some apparent good? These were the sorts of questions that prodded Kant toward his categorical imperative.

The First Principle of Moral Reasoning

Thomas does not turn to a categorical imperative. Still, he insists that the first principle of moral reasoning is "Pursue good and avoid evil"; it is not "If you want the good, then you should pursue it." How does he avoid this conditional command? How does he remove the tentative aspect of the hypothetical imperative? By realizing that the inclination to the good is presupposed to the first moral principle. This inclination is inseparable from our human nature. With our wills we always desire the human good. If you are a human being, which you are if you are reading this, then you are inclined to the human good, and if you are inclined to the good, then you should pursue it. Just as we might transform the conditional "If someone is building a house, then he should lay the foundation first" into the simple statement, "House builders should lay the foundation first," so we can transform "If someone is inclined to the human good, then he should pursue it" into "Human beings should pursue the human good."

Aquinas is not so naive as to suppose that everyone always wants the true good. Murderers, thieves, gluttons, and so on, have all developed the habit of seeking some apparent good rather than the true good. Of course, even these people still desire the *formality* of the good; that is, they perceive everything they seek (even if mistakenly) as in some manner good. The glutton, for instance, pursues animal pleasures as if they were good, although for a human being they are not truly fulfilling. "Pursue the good," however, does not mean "Pursue things under the formality of goodness." We cannot help but do that. Rather, it means "Pursue what is truly good," or "Pursue what is humanly good." We can fail from this precept, and we sometimes do.

Still, we all do want fulfillment, which can be found only in the human good, so we readily perceive that we should pursue the human good. But when we sin or offend against the good we get caught up in the fulfillment of some errant desire. Rather than seeking human fulfillment, we seek the fulfillment of this particular desire. In a kind of absurdity we say, "Yes, I know that I should seek fulfillment, but at the moment I just want this thing here instead." We choose to care less about our fulfillment because we would prefer to satisfy some particularly pressing desire. What we end up pursuing still has the formality of the good, for to fulfill this desire is the good of something, but it does not have the formality of the human good (*Summa contra Gentiles* III, 9, #1).

The more a person develops a habit for some vice, the more his preferences become distorted, and so his judgment also becomes more distorted. At some point he becomes willing to throw out the first principle of moral reasoning. He becomes so obsessed with his dominant passion that he finds it difficult to understand why anyone would seek human fulfillment in preference to his passions. He understands that he should pursue the human good, but he has given up the idea that he should pursue the human good alone, or that he should pursue the human good above all. Other goods seem more worthwhile to him. He never forgets, however, that he has abandoned the true good for a false good; it's just that the false good seems so much better to him. He is troubled at times, I suppose, by the realization that he is acting irrationally, but he cannot imagine acting any other way.

Has such a person, then, opted out of morals? By giving up the desire for true fulfillment, preferring rather the fulfillment of some particular desire, has he escaped the first principle of moral reasoning the way that someone might escape the command "Train hard" by abandoning his desire to win the race? Yes and no. Yes, he has decided that the precept shall have no force in his life, since he does not desire the human end enough. No, for he cannot remove the yearning for fulfillment, which will be realized only by following the first principle of moral reasoning. He will continue to feed his passion, with ever-diminishing returns. His desire for fulfillment will only increase, yet it will never be sated, for he has not changed his nature. As we will see next chapter, he is still human, with human capacities that cannot be filled through the goods he pursues. His potential will be forever cheated. Even if he is clear-sighted enough to perceive this truth, however, he will not likely abandon his obsession, for he has learned to prefer it to the true good. The precept "Pursue the human good" will always lurk in the background as the only means to fulfillment, but he will nevertheless obey the command "Pursue this good instead."

From Truth to Truth

The whole of ethics is united by the principle that we should pursue good and avoid evil. This principle does not, however, contain all of ethics. It is not enough to know that we should pursue the good; in addition, we must know in what the good is found. Such is the role of more particular precepts of what Aquinas calls the natural law, that is, the moral law. Simply knowing that we should pursue the human good does not tell us that we should seek the truth, for we must first know that understanding the truth constitutes part of the human good. Similarly, we must come to understand that the human good should be shared with others, that our emotions should be guided by reason, and so on. While these precepts are still glaringly general, they are nevertheless more specific than the first principle. They provide content not found in the first principle of moral reasoning. Aquinas says, therefore, that morality requires more than a single precept, but that nevertheless all of the precepts are united by the overarching first precept (I-II, 94, 2).

The sum of these precepts constitutes the natural law. It is a law because it provides rational direction of our actions to the good. It is natural both because it finds its source in our natural inclinations and because it is known through the natural ability of our minds, without the assistance of divine revelation. We can know moral truths even without revealed religion. It is a law of human behavior, showing us the way to attain the good.

From these general principles of the natural law we move to further moral knowledge, reaching conclusions about more particular obligations (I-II, 95, 2). From the idea that we should not harm others, we derive the precept that we should not backbite, or that we should not kill. From our knowledge that we should be fair, and that physical appearance is not (usually) a relevant basis for different treatment, we conclude that we should not discriminate based upon color of skin. From our realization that we should desire rationally, we conclude that we should not be attached to material possessions, or that we should not be envious.

These derivations sometimes result in confusion, for human beings are prone to err, and they often distort moral truths, reaching unwarranted conclusions. Someone might conclude, for instance, that he can kill an unborn baby, if he judges that the baby is not a rational animal. Or some nations, says Aquinas, have concluded that it is acceptable to steal from others outside their tribe. These widespread confusions have two sources: errant desires and poor reasoning, sometimes arising from one's culture (I-II, 94, 6). Amidst the confusion we can often see the underlying perception of truth. Indeed, often the confusion rests on what we call "matters of fact," rather than upon moral truths. Western society, for instance, disagrees with the Hindu reverence for cows. An examination of the issue reveals that the two societies have a similar moral understanding, but they disagree over matters of fact. Both societies agree that we should respect rational or spiritual nature, they disagree over whether a cow has such a spiritual nature.

When moral confusion arises from vice, then little can be done to correct it. As we have seen, the vicious person is willing to throw off the first principle of moral reasoning, but long before that he is likely to abandon the more particular precepts. Indeed, he will flatter himself that he is truly pursuing what is good and doing what is fair, just, and reasonable, although deep down he knows that it is not so. Only when he is far progressed in his vice will he candidly reject these precepts as unworthy of his coveted goals, although even then he is likely to keep a public show of upholding these principles; after all, the wicked usually find it useful to be thought good and just. Their case would not be heard if they argued openly for injustice. They must, therefore, argue injustice in the guise of justice. In so doing they give rise to disagreement on fundamental moral principles. We must realize, however, that this disagreement arises not from a defect in our ability to know the truth but from distorted desires.

Confusion might also arise from a poor upbringing, from the training we receive at the hands of our culture. This cultural confusion, we have already seen, might have its roots in rationalization, for whole societies can rationalize a desire or a behavior. At any rate, society can confuse our perception of moral truth, just as poor mathematical training might confuse our understanding of mathematics.

Knowing the Moral Law

How, then, do we come to understand moral truths? We begin by understanding what is our human good, which we grasp by realizing our human capacities or inclinations. When we realize that we are more than mere animals, that we have the capacity to reason, then we see that our good includes acting rationally rather than acting upon impulse; we see that our good includes understanding the truth or that it involves sharing the good with others. From this awareness, certain natural desires of the will arise, from which we come to perceive the human good in our human or voluntary actions. Given these many human goods, we realize that we should pursue these goods, for good is attained only by pursuit. Further reflection helps us to understand more particular directives of how to live our lives.

Of course, we have seen that some people can seek what is only apparently good. They can reject the human good because they prefer some lesser good, such as pleasure or wealth. Even then, their true good remains the same. They have not changed their nature, the fundamental capacities or inclinations that direct them to the true good. They have merely changed their wants. And even their wants have a certain fixture to them, for while they pursue misguided goods, they are still seeking what they suppose to be good. As we have seen in chapter 5, every person, in all that he does, must seek the good. If he rejects the human end in an attempt to free himself from the moral precepts, he is cheating only himself. He may have thrown off the moral law, but he has also thrown off his heart's true longing, the true human good. In short, the moral law is simply the law of true human fulfillment. Follow it, and you will attain your ultimate goal. Transgress it, and you lose the only good that can satisfy the human heart.

Morality is not some burden placed on us from outside, from some divine lawgiver who takes pleasure in controlling our lives. Rather, it springs from our very nature, from who we truly are. We have a place to fill in the universe; we have a direction impressed upon our very being, a purpose that leads us to the end we are meant to realize. We should want, then, to do our part, to fill the potential for which we were made. We should welcome the natural moral law as our light and our guide, as the very road upon which we walk to our ultimate destination. Rather than reject the precepts of the natural law, viewing them as shackles to escape from, we should embrace them as the guide to the very good we seek.

14

Ethics and Happiness

~

It is plain then how wretched is the happiness of mortal life which neither endures for ever with men of calm mind, nor ever wholly delights the care-ridden. Wherefore, then, O mortal men, seek you that happiness without, which lies within yourselves? You are confounded by error and ignorance. I will show you as shortly as I may, the pole on which turns the highest happiness.

Anicius Manlius Severinus Boethius

It is the nature of desire not to be satisfied, and most men live only for the gratification of it.

Aristotle

Why Be Moral?

We are now prepared to answer Glaucon's and Thrasymachus's question. Which way of life is the happier and more profitable, the unjust life or the just life? You will recall that Thrasymachus thought that the unjust life was happier, because the perfectly unjust man is never caught, he becomes the ruler of his city, he is well liked by everyone, and he achieves all that he hopes for. The perfectly just man, on the other hand, has a reputation for injustice; people do not like him but despise him, so that in the end he is falsely accused and found guilty, finally being put to death. Socrates challenged Thrasymachus's view, arguing instead that since justice was a strength, a kind of virtue, it could only help in attaining the good life.

The debate between the two is hardly what we might call academic. It impinges upon the heart of our daily lives. Indeed, we often ask ourselves Thrasymachus's question. Suppose, for instance, that as I stand in the bank holding on to the money given me by the teller, I take counsel and reach the judgment that I should return the extra twenty dollars. Before I move on to the act of command, I hesitate and say, "But what's in it for me? Sure, it is the morally right thing to do, but I get nothing out of it. Why should I bother being moral anyway?" I would have voiced a basic rejection of moral truth, rejecting not merely this particular precept or that particular virtue; rather, I would have thrown out the whole of morality. Indeed, I would have thrown out the very idea of morality, supposing that I stand above it, and that I can take it or leave it; it has no binding force upon me, but is merely some sort of game that I can choose to play or not. If there is nothing in it for me, then why play it?

At the beginning of this book we already suggested a response to this line of reasoning. We said that ethics simply is the study of our actions insofar as they contribute to the good life. We all want to lead a happy and fulfilling life, and we would all be willing to listen to sound advice on how to do so. That advice is found in ethics. Why, then, should we reject ethics in favor of self-interest? The very thing we want out of life is found in ethics itself. Throughout this book we have tried to indicate ways in which the ethical life is indeed the good life. We suggested, for instance, that blind passions do not satisfy; we suggested that our deepest desires are found in the will; and we suggested that happiness is not found in some solitary private accomplishment but only in union with others.

Still, we have a hankering to free ourselves from morality, as if it were a burden preventing us from achieving happiness. We cannot quite shake off the idea that morality is opposed to our own self-interest, that we might be better off if we didn't have to follow this set of rules. We see a dichotomy between the moral life and the happy life. The moral life is a matter of following the moral rules, doing the right thing. The happy life, on the other hand, is a matter of satisfying our desires, doing what we want to do. These two, it seems, often come in conflict with one another, for inevitably we sometimes desire what is against the rules. If we choose to follow the rules, then we are not satisfying our desires but are giving up the happy life. On the other hand, if we choose to satisfy our desire then we have chosen the happy life but have abandoned the moral life. If forced to decide between the two ways of life, then, the choice seems straightforward: we all want to be happy, but why should we lead the moral life? What could possibly induce us to give up happiness for a set of rules?

The Good Life

The course of this book has been an attempt to answer this difficulty. It has been a self-help guide to what is truly fulfilling of us as human beings. We have seen that the good life depends upon what we are. We are not mere grasshoppers, but human beings with reason and will, with emotions that can share in the light of reason; we are not solitary animals, but we pursue our goals together with others, developing intimate friendships with some. Therefore, we will not be satisfied by mere sensation, by pleasure, or by material wealth. We will be satisfied only by fulfilling our truly human capacities of reason and will. We must follow reason rather than blind emotional desire. We must seek the spiritual goods of love of others, friendship, justice, and the understanding of the truth. If we neglect these human capacities, and seek only to gratify our emotions apart from reason, then we will never be truly satisfied. We will be attempting to live the life of a pig within the body and mind of a human being. It cannot be done. The pig's life will ever prove empty to us who have the potential for so much more.

We all judge our lives and our actions in the light of happiness. Or, to remove some of the taint of selfishness associated with the word "happiness," we might say that we all want the good life, a life that need not be selfish but could be a life of sacrificing for others. We cannot divide our actions into those in which we act for happiness and those in which we act for something else, such as morality. In all that we do we seek the good life; we always pursue fulfillment. Of course, we don't always attain it. We make mistakes. We pursue misguided goals; we choose inadequate means. Still, we always *want* fulfillment. Wouldn't it be good, then, if we knew how to achieve it?

The philosopher Aristotle compares us to two archers (*Nichomachean Ethics*, bk. 1, ch. 2). Both are seeking to hit some target, but the first one knows where the target is, while the second one does not. Clearly, the first archer has the better chance of hitting the target, for the second will hit the mark only by pure luck. Unfortunately, suggests Aristotle, we are all too often like the second archer. We are aiming at some goal—for we all want fulfillment out of life—but we don't know what it is. We go about our lives seeking one thing and then another, and yet another, in a kind of rat race that has no end. We all want something out of life, but we don't have a clear idea of what. We have never taken the time to reflect and ask, "What is it all about?" We are not very likely, then, to hit our target. Wouldn't it be better if we were like the first archer? Wouldn't it be better if we took some time to reflect and ask what we really want out of life? Then we would be more likely to hit our target.

Aristotle does not mean simply that we must become clear on what our goals are. He means that we must become clear on what is the right goal. It does no good to take careful aim at an oak tree when the true prize is the deer. Similarly, it does little good if after self-examination we decide that what we really want out of life is money. We might be clear on our goal, but we would not be clear on the right goal, for money will not satisfy the human heart.

Aristotle and Aquinas, then, reject the popular notion that happiness is what you make it. On this view, each person has his own set of desires, and so each person has his own happiness. What I pursue in hopes of happiness may not interest you, and what you seek, I might despise. Some find happiness in wealth, others in power. Still, others find happiness in a quiet family life. Some find happiness by carousing and licentiousness. Others are happy through the pursuit of knowledge. Some are happy only when they are famous. According to this position—rejected by Aquinas—each of us wants something different out of life, so each of us will find happiness in something different. Happiness is simply a matter of achieving our goals, whatever they may be. Different goals make for different happinesses.

Nothing could be more un-American than to claim, as Aquinas does, that some people are simply mistaken in their pursuit of happiness; they are aiming at the wrong goal, and even should they attain it, they will not be happy. We don't like happiness being dictated to us. While we can accept (somewhat begrudgingly) being told what is right or wrong, we cannot endure being told what is good for us. Objective morality is understandable—at least for things like racism or tolerance—but an objectively identifiable good life is simple nonsense. How can anyone else tell me what will make me happy?

Yet haven't we all experienced disappointment when we have achieved our dearest goals? Haven't we pursued some object as if it would make us happy, worked hard to achieve it, and yet when finally we attained it we were disillusioned? That new car didn't really satisfy us, that exotic pleasure was a letdown, and that new job still left us yearning for more. Cannot we be mistaken in the goals we set? Of course we can. Our desires are not magical; they do not confer upon the thing desired the ability to make us happy. Our desires are as fallible as anything else about us. Sometimes we desire things truly worthy of pursuit; at other times we desire what can never really satisfy us. Happiness, then, cannot simply be setting goals and achieving them, for we can set the wrong goals. Happiness must be attaining the right goals. We should take the time to reflect, then, upon what goals are truly worthy of pursuit.

False Happiness

Not all of the goals that people set for themselves will satisfy the human heart. Pleasure, for instance, will never satisfy the human longing, and those who set pleasure as the ultimate goal of their lives will never attain happiness (I-II, 2, 6). Pleasure, then, is better called a false happiness; it is something that people pursue as if it would make them happy, but ultimately it does not. Similarly, says Aquinas, wealth and power, fame and glory, are only false happinesses (I-II, 2). If we are to hit the target, we must be archers who know what true happiness is.

Of course we all want pleasure, but some people set up pleasure as the thing they really want out of life, as the ultimate goal that they suppose will make them happy. These people will never find happiness, for the human heart is not satisfied by mere animal pleasure. This dissatisfaction of the human heart is revealed in the ever more twisted ways that pleasure is pursued. Animal pursuit of pleasure is pretty straightforward, even if it is sometimes surprising, but the human pursuit of pleasure ranges from the silly to the grotesque. Why? Because our hearts are not made to be satisfied by pleasure, and those who set their sights on pleasure begin to twist it in hope that something a little different will finally satisfy. But it never does, because the only truly satisfying pleasures are those that conform to reason, which discovers the true goods in things. Pleasure by itself is a false happiness; reasonable pleasure can be part of true happiness.

A similar phenomenon arises for material wealth (I-II, 2, 1). Again, we all want some possessions, at least the bare necessities, and we all know some people who set their hearts on wealth as if it would make them happy. But wealth by its very nature, says Aquinas, is directed as a means toward our good; it itself is not the good, but is for the sake of the good. Put simply, wealth is something we use. We use money to buy things; we use the things we buy for some activity. Wealth, then, is not an ultimate end, but something directed toward the end. Those who pursue wealth as if it were the ultimate goal are deceived, and they will never be satisfied. If we observe those who set their hearts on wealth we see that they indeed are not satisfied. They always seek more; indeed, the more they have, the more they seem to want.

Aquinas says that we can always imagine something satisfying us. This imagination gives rise to desire. When the reality is achieved, however, we can no longer rely upon imagination but are faced with the reality, which does not satisfy. As a result, we go searching for more in our imagination. Someone imagines, for instance, that he will be happy if only he has a million dollars. When he acquires the money, however, he realizes that he is not satisfied. He then imagines that he would be happy if only he had two million dollars. When this extra money is acquired he must puff up his imagination even more. Since two million dollars does not satisfy, perhaps he needs five million. And so it goes. The more he has, the more he must expand his ideas of what will bring him happiness. The more he has, the more he desires to have.

Power, too, is only a false happiness (I-II, 2, 4). Those who seek power as an ultimate goal are doomed to dissatisfaction, for like wealth, power is to be used to attain other goals. Furthermore, its use can be for either good or evil; of itself, therefore, it is not simply a good.

Fame or glory is also only an illusory happiness (I-II, 2 and 3). It is the recognition by others of the good we possess. Someone famous for singing is recognized as a great singer; someone famous for acting is recognized as a great actor; and so on. But if fame is a mere recognition of a good, then it cannot possibly be more important than the good recognized. The ultimate goal should be the good possessed, rather than the recognition of it. We should want the talent of singing more than the recognition of our talent; we should want to be a good actor more than the recognition of our acting. Those who set their hearts on fame get matters mixed up. They want the recognition more than the good. As a result, they tend to become fakes, putting on a show of goodness, so that others will praise them.

Those who pursue these misguided goods may not recognize their error. They may emphatically insist that they are happy, their vehemence perhaps meant more to persuade themselves than anyone else. We have seen that what appears good to someone depends upon his disposition. To a miser, wealth appears good; to a serial killer, the act of killing appears satisfying. The miser, then, least of all will perceive the error of his ways. The wealth he accumulates will never satisfy his heart, but nevertheless he will assume that the problem is not in the wealth. "If only I had more," he will say to himself, "then I would be happy." As long as his heart is set upon possessions, he will judge that these, and these alone, will bring him happiness. He will always say to himself that he needs more money. He will never say that perhaps he needs something different, true friendship, care for others, or some such thing.

We should not be led astray by these faulty judgments, concluding that happiness is relative to our desires and goals. Certainly, people's judgment of the good life is relative to their desires. But their desires may themselves be misguided or even perverse. Why should we accept the judgment of a greedy or vainglorious person? Should we not, rather, recognize that their disagreeable personalities have corrupted their judgments, preventing them from perceiving the true good?

True Happiness

True happiness will not be found in any of these goods, for the human heart is made for greater things. Upon what goal, then, should we set our sights? Upon those things that are fully human, that realize our true capacities as human beings, for only through these will our desires be filled. We must lead a human life and not the life of a pig. We are beings with the capacity to understand the truth through reason, with the ability to love one another through our wills. Should we settle, then, for mere pleasure? Should we settle for material possessions, or for the illusions of fame? Or should we, rather, seek to lead a human life of reason and love? We will attain happiness only by performing well our peculiarly human activity of reason.

Such is Aristotle's doctrine on happiness, and Thomas's as well, although he will add a supernatural element. A caricature of this teaching would have the life of reason, and so the happy life, be a life spent reading books, meditating, and doing philosophy. The truly happy person, on this reading, is Rodin's *Thinker,* the sculpture of a man staring intently into empty space.

Throughout this book we have seen, however, that the life of reason is much richer and much more complex. Certainly, contemplation of the truth is an important part of the life of reason. Indeed, for Aquinas it has a priority; it is that to which the others are directed and which puts order into all the others (I-II, 3, 5 and 6). We as human beings can understand the truth, so we should not remain mere animals, pursuing various means of survival, but should seek to understand the world around us and its creator. We alone can grasp the truth, so part of human happiness is found in this activity. The intellectual virtues are essential to the happy life; that does not mean that everyone must be an intellectual, but everyone must love the truth and its pursuit.

Nor should we neglect the practical intellectual virtues, for we have seen that reason does more than understand the truth. With it we can also develop certain skills. A doctor, for instance, uses her reason to heal; a computer programmer uses his reason to accomplish his work; and so on. Just about any human skill, from fishing to teaching, involves the use of reason. We perform our human activity well, then, not only by sitting and gazing, like Rodin's *Thinker,* but also by doing, by engaging our mind in the tasks before us. Here, too, we are not mere animals, acting purely on instinct and conditioning, but can use our understanding to be creative.

When it comes to using our minds to direct our activities, we cannot forget prudence, which sets our own actions in order to the goal of our life. This use of reason also belongs to the life of reason. Unlike animals that act upon unreflective instinct, we can plan and work to achieve the goal of our life.

Yet more must be included in the life of reason. For we have seen that the will, as well as reason, is a peculiarly human capacity. We alone can love the true good, and we alone can love others with a true love of friendship. The perfection of the will, then, must also be included within the life of reason. That perfection includes the virtue of justice—which seeks the right relation to others—and a more intimate love with our closer friends.

We have also seen that the emotions themselves belong to the life of reason, for human emotions are not mere animal emotions. Our desires not only can respond to the presentations of the imagination but also can conform to the judgments of reason. Our emotions can be either reasonable or unreasonable. They can be formed by that peculiarly rational capacity, found especially in the virtue of prudence, which directs activities toward an end. Our emotions, then, share in reason, and so become part of the life of reason.

A Mold or a Model?

Part of our repugnance to the notion of an objectively identifi-able good life is that it seems to force us into a mold. If only one single happy life applies to all human beings, then where is variety? Must I live my life exactly like everyone else if I am to be happy? Cannot I choose my own life? Cannot I live my life dif-ferently from others and yet be happy?

We can now see that this repugnance arises more from a caricature of Aquinas than from Aquinas himself. Thomas is not saying that we must all be philosophers if we want to be happy. He is saying that we must lead the life of reason. The life of reason, however, is far from a mold. It has an openness and flexibility about it that leaves plenty of room for variety and choice, making it more of a model than a mold. Are we to un-derstand the truth? Yes, indeed. But the truth is vast, and no one can comprehend it all. We each can choose to understand that part of the truth that is most appealing to us. Some will find philosophy interesting, others mathematics, others history, and still others science. Are we to develop certain skills? Yes, indeed. But no one can be good at everything, so we may choose which skills to develop. Some will choose to become good at car-pentry, others at medicine, others at business, and still others at music. There is no straitjacket here. Should we love others and seek a just community? Certainly. But we can still choose our particular friends; we can still choose with whom we engage in business. That business must be just, of course, but such a limi-tation is hardly a mold but more of a model. Must our emotions follow the guidance of reason? Yes, indeed. But that still leaves plenty of room for diversity of personality. Some people will be outgoing, others reserved; some will be cheerful, others more solemn. The guide of reason is not always fixed in stone, but has room for personal judgment. True, no one must desire to commit adultery. But some people may desire to marry and others not. Those that desire to marry may desire this particular woman or that particular man.

The life of reason is hardly an oppressive mold that inhibits diversity. No doubt it places restrictions and limitations, but mostly it sets an ideal that may be achieved in a variety of ways. Indeed, human variety is itself necessary to fill out all that is implied in the life of reason. If we lived isolated lives, without sharing the rich diversity of others, we would not fully realize our human potential.

Happiness and God

Someone might protest that all of this talk of the life of reason is not Thomas's teaching of the good life, for he says that happiness can be found in God alone. No created good can ever fulfill our needs. Only the uncreated God, who is complete and perfect goodness, can bring us happiness (I-II, 2, 8).

Such indeed is Aquinas's view. But the God of happiness cannot remain distant and separate from us. If he is to bring us happiness, we must possess him; we must attain him as the goal of our lives. On this point, Aquinas distinguishes between a good and its possession. If wealth is the good, then it must yet be possessed, for someone else's wealth hardly satisfies our needs. If truth is the good, then we must yet acquire the truth, which we do through understanding. Similarly, if God is the good, then he must yet be attained by us (I-II, 1, 8; I-II, 3, 1).

How can we attain God? In one sense, he can never be attained in this life but only in the next. Only in heaven will we see God face to face and so attain to the good we seek. According to some interpreters of Aquinas, *only* in this sense can we attain God. Apart from the life of heaven, which is a supernatural gift of God, our natural longings are destined to be frustrated. Apart from heaven, human nature is made in vain. We must differ from these interpreters, however, for Aquinas grants a participated happiness that can be attained in this life. It may not be the fullness of happiness, but it is happiness in the proper sense of the word (I-II, 3, 2, ad 4; I-II, 3, 6; I-II, 5, 3, especially ad 2; I-II, 5, 5).

We attain to God in this life by becoming like him and by knowing and loving him insofar as we are able. Consider how a picture captures the beauty of the landscape it portrays. It reflects the original beauty, and thereby shares in it. Similarly, we are like a divine work of art, which can reflect the beauty of God and so share in his good (*Summa contra Gentiles*, III, 19 & 20). All of creation cries out the glory of God in some manner (I, 5, 1, ad 2). Some creatures reflect merely the existence of God; others the eternal life of God; still others, the ability to know. Only human beings, however, reflect the knowledge of God itself, for through the visible things around us we can come to understand their invisible source. We alone can know God, and we alone can love him in himself. Just as God understands and loves, so can we understand and love through our reason and will.

Indeed, in our knowledge of God we possess him more immediately than through a mere reflection, for by knowing him we attain to God himself (I-II, 1, 8). This imperfect human knowledge has many inadequacies. It never achieves a knowledge of God as he is in himself, but only through his reflection in creation; it never is whole and entire, but only partial and bit by bit. But nevertheless, it is knowledge of God. Human nature is not in vain, then, for it attains to God in the manner it is able, which is always imperfectly. That we should also someday be able to possess God fully in the vision of heaven is something far beyond what our nature could aspire to. On a natural level, we do seek the knowledge of God, but only as we can attain it, which is bit by bit.

Happiness is indeed found in God alone, but human happiness is found in possessing God, which we do through our activities, primarily through our activities of knowing and loving. Only by living a fully human life, a life of reason and the virtues, do we truly reflect God's good and so share in it, for only then do we ourselves become good. We reflect the overflowing actuality of God by realizing our own potential. In other words, there is not such a great divide between Aristotle's life of reason and Aquinas's possession of God, at least on the natural level. By living out the life of reason we come to possess God in this life. As Aristotle says, we must develop that divine element within us (*Nichomachean Ethics*, bk. 10, ch. 7).

The Moral Life

Let us not lose sight of Thrasymachus. Let us not lose sight of those who urge us to abandon morality so that we may then satisfy our desires. What are we to say to these people? We must insist that they are drawing a false dichotomy; the moral life and the happy life are not separate, but they are one and the same. By leading a moral life we are also leading a happy life, for the happy life is none other than the life of reason, which in turn includes the virtues within it. Do we wish to be happy? Then let us control our emotions, guiding them according to the judgment of reason. Do we wish to be moral? Then let us do the same. Do we think that we will attain happiness by neglecting our will while we gratify our emotions? We are mistaken, for the truly human life includes justice and the intimate love of friendship. The virtue of practical wisdom, too, belongs to the happy life, for it is part of our creative activity, putting order into our own actions. We have already seen how the intellectual virtues fit into the moral life. They are not necessary, but the right desire for them is.

In the end, the moral life is inseparable from the life of reason, and the life of reason, which is the happy life, is inseparable from the moral life. We cannot be happy by rejecting our humanity and leading the life of animals. We cannot be happy by exalting our individual good and rejecting the divine good reflected in others. Happiness will be found only in the moral life, and those that lead a moral life will find in it their happiness.

The Satisfaction of Desire

Still, doesn't ethics—and the life of reason—demand that we make sacrifices, giving up our own good for the sake of others, at times denying our desires? The virtue of moderation, for instance, requires that we check our desires when they would seek that of which reason disapproves. Is not the life of reason, then, opposed to the happy life, which seeks to satisfy our desires? The life of reason may fulfill our various rational capacities, but it does not satisfy all our wants, and at times it directly denies them. The life of happiness, on the other hand, is surely a life in which our desires are satisfied. How could we say that we are happy, however rational our lives might be, if our desires were left unsatisfied?

In response to this objection, Thomas would insist that the life of reason is indeed the most satisfying of lives. Certainly, the life of reason will not satisfy all our desires. It will, for instance, oppose our unreasonable emotions. At the same time, however, the life of reason satisfies other of our desires. Recall that we are complex animals with a great diversity of desires. We have many emotional desires, including desires for food, sex, friendship, security, popularity, and so on. Many of our desires, such as those for the latest technological marvels, are not necessary or natural, but we have chosen to acquire them. On top of these we have desires of the will, those spiritual desires that can seek the true good of others. Now amidst this complex tangle of desires, it should be little wonder that we will not always be able to fulfill every desire. But we might, at least, satisfy those desires that are deepest and most basic.

These basic desires are found not in a hierarchy of needs, but in the spiritual desires of the will. With the will we love the true good; we love not just this particular good here or that particular good there, but goodness itself; we love the complete good, a good that is found in God. By comparison to the emotions the longings of the will are fathomless. The emotions are but tiny fleas upon a mammoth of an elephant, which is the will (I-II, 2, 6). The will, being a spiritual capacity, has a longing not for any finite good, but for goodness itself, for the infinite good that is God. Should we, then, feed the fleas and let the elephant go hungry?

Unfortunately, we often pay more attention to the emotions, which are more evident to us, than to the will. We go about our lives placating this feeling, that feeling, and the next, each emotion as it arises demanding its gratification. We hardly have time to notice that all the while our deeper longings, which do not press upon our senses, are being left unsatisfied. Why is a culture such as our own, which has spent all in the pursuit of worldly goods and pleasures, haunted by an angst, an ennui of the heart? Why are suicides so prevalent; why is everyone running off to psychological treatment; and why do we always need more, more, more? Because we have missed the boat. We have sought to gratify our emotions at the expense of our will.

"Our hearts are restless until they rest in You," said St. Augustine to God (*Confessions,* bk. 1, ch. 1), and though we will not fully rest in God during this life, we can have some participation in the divine life. We must, says Aristotle, develop that divine element within us (*Nichomachean Ethics,* bk. 10, ch. 7). We must lead the life of reason, attaining to the beauty of God himself, and so satisfy the yearnings of the will. Only by attaining to God, in whatever degree we are able, can our hearts ever be satisfied. That this natural reflection of God should be superseded by a greater and fuller participation in the life of God, Aristotle would never know. Aquinas did know. He knew that stopping with the life of reason was insufficient. The extent of this book, however, is to consider what we can know of morals only through the use of our natural reason. We can only point to the supernatural life, which is a sharing in the life of Christ.

What of those emotional desires that must at times be left unsatisfied? Does this dissatisfaction make us unhappy, thereby separating the moral life and the happy life? It should not. These desires are themselves disordered. They are inappropriate desires, longings for what is not truly good. They indicate some defect in us in need of correction. To gratify them is to bring dissatisfaction to the will, for the will is naturally repelled by what is evil. If our heart is in the right place, keeping that unity of purpose and decisiveness necessary for the act of command, then we will endure these dissatisfactions of the emotions for the much greater satisfaction of the will. True self-love, says Aquinas, seeks the good of reason, and not the good of the emotions (II-II, 25, 4, ad 3).

Besides, the moral life can bring these desires in order. Are you now disappointed that you must sacrifice sexual satisfaction for the sake of the moral life? It need not always be so. Recall that we can change our desires over time, bringing them under the guidance of reason. Rather than say, "I cannot have this pleasure, therefore, I will be unhappy," we should say, "I cannot satisfy this desire, therefore, I will get rid of it." In the end, we will leave no desire unsatisfied, for we will develop only those desires that are in accord with the life of reason. Realistically, of course, we must recognize that our desires for evil will never entirely disappear; they will always be with us. Still, we can at least diminish them. And when they do torment us we can set our hearts on higher things, on the things of God.

The moral life is indeed the happy life, the satisfaction of our desires. The deepest satisfaction is found in God alone.

SELECTED BIBLIOGRAPHY

English Translations of Some of Aquinas's Writings

Aquinas, Thomas. *The Disputed Questions on Truth*. Chicago: H. Regnery, 1952.
———. *On Evil*. Notre Dame, Ind.: University of Notre Dame Press, 1995.
———. *Summa contra Gentiles*. Notre Dame, Ind.: University of Notre Dame Press, 1975.
———. *Summa theologiae: Latin Text and English Translation, Introductions, Notes, Appendices, and Glossaries*. Cambridge: Blackfriars, 1964.
Pegis, Anton C. *Basic Writings of Saint Thomas Aquinas*. New York: Random House, 1945.

Other Books on the Thought of Aquinas

Chesterton, G. K. *St. Thomas Aquinas*. San Francisco: Ignatius Press, 2002.
Kreeft, Peter. *Back to Virtue: Traditional Moral Wisdom for Modern Moral Confusion*. San Fransisco: Ignatius Press, 1992.
McInerny, Ralph. *Aquinas on Human Action: A Theory of Practice*. Washington, D.C.: The Catholic University of America Press. 1997.
———. *Ethica Thomistica: The Moral Philosophy of Thomas Aquinas*. Rev. ed. Washington, D.C.: The Catholic University of America Press, 1997.
———. *A First Glance at Saint Thomas Aquinas: A Handbook for Peeping Thomists*. Notre Dame, Ind.: University of Notre Dame Press, 1990.
———. *Saint Thomas Aquinas*. Notre Dame, Ind.: University of Notre Dame Press, 1982.
O'Donnell, Robert A. *Hooked on Philosophy: Thomas Aquinas Made Easy*. New York: Alba House, 1995.
Pieper, Josef. *A Brief Reader on the Virtues of the Human Heart*. San Francisco: Ignatius Press. 1991.

————. *The Four Cardinal Virtues.* Notre Dame, Ind.: University of Notre Dame Press, 1966.

————. *A Guide to Thomas Aquinas.* San Francisco: Ignatius Press, 1991.

————. *Leisure: The Basis of Culture.* South Bend, Ind.: St. Augustine's Press, 1998.

Torrell, Jean-Pierre. *Saint Thomas Aquinas.* Washington, D.C.: The Catholic University of America Press, 1996.

INDEX

Living the Good Life: A Beginner's Thomistic Ethics was designed and typeset in Scala with Aquiline display type by Kachergis Book Design of Pittsboro, North Carolina. It was printed on 60-pound Naturals Recycled and bound by McNaughton & Gunn of Saline, Michigan.